WILD FOWL DECOYS

~ CHESAPEAKE BAY CANVAS-BACK ~

SUSQUEHANNA FLATS ABOUT 1880.

WILD FOWL DECOYS

BY JOEL BARBER

THE DERRYDALE PRESS

LANHAM AND NEW YORK

THE DERRYDALE PRESS

Published in the United States of America
by The Derrydale Press
4720 Boston Way, Lanham, Maryland 20706

Distributed by NATIONAL BOOK NETWORK, INC.

Original Derrydale printing 1934
First paperback printing with french folds 2000

ISBN 1-56833-145-2 (pbk. : alk. paper)

™ The paper used in this publication meets the minimum requirements of
American National Standard for Information Sciences—Permanence of
Paper for Printed Library Materials, ANSI/NISO Z39.48-1992.
Manufactured in the United States of America.

TO MY SONS
D. S. B. *and* J. G. B.

ACKNOWLEDGMENT

IN GATHERING MATERIAL *for this book, I have had the help of many friends—some connections of long standing, others made in passing, but all generous with what they had to give. Now—through process of publication, the courtesy of these friends becomes Sportsman History. It is a great pleasure to acknowledge indebtedness and thank them all.*

AUTHOR

Contents

CONTENTS
PART VI

Illustrations

ILLUSTRATIONS

ILLUSTRATIONS

[xiii]

ILLUSTRATIONS

ILLUSTRATIONS

WILD FOWL DECOYS

THE AUTHOR

LEGEND

A LONG TIME AGO an American Indian had a swell idea. He was a fowler—one whose quarry passed swiftly and beyond range of his primitive weapons. And so he thought to invent a lure, an invitation for all wild waterfowl to foregather at hunter's ambush.

The new device was fashioned in the likeness of duck; an artificial Canvas-back, made of reeds and feathers and colored by native paints. The man cut and tried—and tried again. He made one. He made two. Finally there were seven and when tethered on the water, they floated for all the world like a group of wild ducks feeding.

North America was a wilderness then—a land of forests and streams. Over trackless plains, buffalo grass stood high and virgin. In silent mountains lay gold unsought. There were no White Men. The vast continent was untilled, unfenced and uninhabited save for roving bands of Indians. And all life was wild; even the people were savage and predatory.

Over this land of solitude, so long ago, lay the hush of autumn. Day was breaking. In the thatch a northerly wind played. Patches of shell ice glinted in the marsh. Silence was broken only by lapping water and whistle of wings on errands of migration.

The wild-fowl of North America were moving southward.

LEGEND

Wisps of snipe had come and gone again. Wild geese passed leisurely in the sky. Over the estuary waterfowl hovered as smoke clings to the sea.

Off shore a few yards, a group of reeded Canvas-backs rode crazily at anchor. Mooring lines of twisted grass pitched downward through waving tendrils to stone anchors on wild celery bottom. Behind a flimsy screen of dried grass the red-skinned inventor shivered in the cold. The idea was launched—to live or die; nebulous but potent as rum.

Time passed. More time—then the great deception raised its head. Nature was to serve a new master. Instinct to foregather, buried deep in the hearts of wild waterfowl, was to meet disaster.

In the distance a swiftly moving flock of birds faltered in the sky. The false Canvas-backs rolled and pitched dully on the water. The Indian crouched lower in the reeds. Tapping in his breast was a gift to posterity—"expectancy!" It touched his hair in the back, rippled across his jaw-bone and down his spine. His knee sank deeper in the matted grass.

Events followed swiftly. The leading birds swung shorewards toward the false ducks on the water; oncoming trailers followed, telescoping and banking on the turn. There was no disorder. Like magic the line of hurtling birds straightened, gathered speed, drove headlong in and set their wings to halt.

They were over the group on the water.

On the shore a bow-string twanged!—then again! and again!

For a moment there was hurried confusion; then bending sharply on stiff wings the visitors fled.

The false Canvas-backs on their stone anchors held steadily into the wind, even at birth intrepid and inscrutable. Beyond them, drifting slowly leeward, two white breasts sprawled loosely in the sea.

It began to snow. In the distance the forest was turning a deeper blue. To right and left the sloping shore was merging with water. In his trampled nest the lone inventor stood back against the waving marsh.

And then it came—the long drawn yell of Indian victory; victory for generations of fowlers to come. The echo of that great idea still vibrates along the migratory paths of all American waterfowl.

Wild ducks had decoyed; were to decoy for evermore. They were never to know and never to understand. For that was a thousand years ago.

NOTE

THE IMPORTANCE *of pictorial records made it advisable to include an unusual number of illustrations in this volume. This prevented placing plates adjacent to references in the text. The reader will find it convenient to refer to the list of illustrations for guidance in locating any plate mentioned in the text.*

PART I

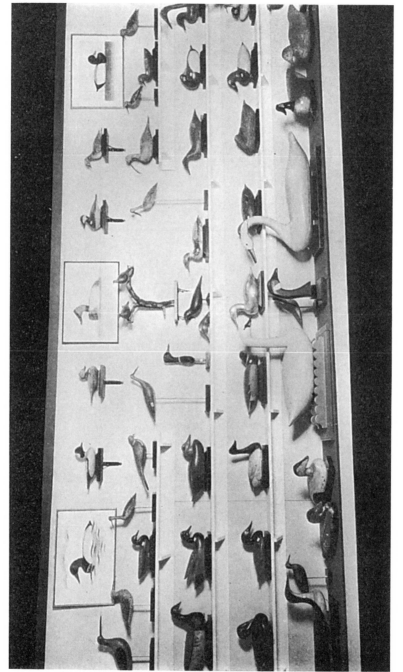

Plate I

PART OF THE AUTHOR'S COLLECTION

On Collecting Decoys

"Go up in the loft," the Captain said,
"And fetch my old decoys" . . .

For some years I have collected old decoys with the idea of writing a book about them—a sort of a decoy duck omnibus with pictures and stories. Sportsmen friends, including a sportsman publisher, encouraged the idea but none of us knew, or could know, what a decoy book would turn out to be.

I am still collecting, still lured and victimized by decoys, but, as search concludes, the material has a queer look about it. References drawn from old books on wild fowling have the familiar convention of history but the part I found has not. I don't know what it has.

Presumably I am not historically minded. It may be that I took the wrong turning. But my search led to a setting of romance, water and water-front. Names were grand and high sounding—Chesapeake, the Great South Bay, waters of Virginia and the Carolinas, up the coast to bays and estuaries of New England and Nova Scotia. But the places I visited were far from grand. The information I sought seemed to lie in out-of-the-way places, in little known tide-water villages, ramshackle boat-yards and along desolate sloping shores. Here, at off seasons and behind the scenes of traditional duck shooting, I collected decoys and data. If what I found is only shanty gossip, I alone am to blame. But to me these places and the men and the things I found there are an integral part of the history of American decoys.

On a visit to Knotts Island, Virginia, for example, I add to my collection a group of old-time Ruddy Duck. They were very old and of singular perfection. As a collector I was elated for Ruddies are among the rarest decoys on the whole Atlantic seaboard. But that does not complete the story.

In the very act of opening the door of the old boathouse where I found them, I recognized historical ground—my kind of history. The Ruddies, six or eight of them, lay forgotten in a corner with miscellaneous gear. Some were broken beyond repair, all were scarred by service and bleached by exposure. Only traces of the original painting remained, but the bottom of each decoy, burned deep on the dead rise, bore the initials—L. D.

L. D. it appeared was the mark of a "Mr. Lee Dudley," one-time professional gunner and celebrated as a decoy maker. With the passing of market shooting, he had sold his rig and retired to a farm on the mainland. So much for bare facts.

It was midwinter and the roads were terrible, but in company with Pax Ewell navigating the "Model T" and my host carrying one of the old Ruddies in his pocket, I called on Mr. Dudley.

The southern boundary of Virginia crosses Knotts Island here, and the object of our visit lay just over the line in the state of North Carolina. Leaving the Ford at the mail box on the stone road, we walked the last half mile to the house. On the right, going in, lay a cotton field, snowlike tufts clinging to bare stalks. On the other side wild looking cattle watched silently from a swampy pasture. In places water covered the road. Overhead buzzards wheeled in the sky. It was very still. Off in the woods at the left, someone was cutting wood, each blow of the axe falling clear and distinct on the winter afternoon.

ON COLLECTING DECOYS

The house stood in a yard enclosed by weather-beaten boarding. A few turkeys perched on the fence; otherwise the place seemed deserted, bleak and meagre. But the yard looked southward over the waters of Currituck. Like the boat-house on the shore, the fence carried a faint tinge of greenish moss. There were no live oaks here but near the house, a black old pine tree whispered steadily in the wind. I was reminded somehow of the gun club on Knotts Island.

Along the wall by the kitchen door, hung a line of ducks, mostly Ruddies, punctuated at the end by a pair of Canvas-backs.

Upon inquiry, we were told that Mr. Dudley was cutting wood, but would be back soon.

And the lady was right. As if in answer to some invisible telegraph, the buzzards perhaps, he shortly made appearance.

Mr. Dudley is a very understanding person. Talk held steadily on ducks and decoys. The old Ruddy started a train of reminiscence covering years of Virginia gunning. I learned first hand of days when Boobies (Ruddy) sold for only five cents apiece, barely enough to pay for "loading the shells"; during the nineties, the price went to a dollar apiece, and the gunners called them "dollar ducks." *

Since becoming a dirt farmer, he had made no decoys. A dilapidated bureau on the porch, however, disclosed a queer collection of left-over decoy heads. They were mostly Canvas-backs, some painted, others in natural wood, but all mellowed by years in their al fresco resting-place. Upon leaving, I was presented with two of them, souvenirs of the visit.

At Mr. Dudley's request the old club decoy was left behind. Months later it arrived in New York, resplendent in new paint after the original pattern of Ruddy painting. It is a rare and very fine decoy, one of my prized possessions. But

* Threatened with complete extinction, all shooting of the famous Ruddy Duck is now prohibited.

in 1913 the whole Dudley rig had been sold to the club at the then prevailing price of fifty cents apiece.

That visit to Knotts Island was to produce other historical items. Further search in the club boat-house brought to light an early Canvas-back of the oversized type, now so familiar on Back Bay. I also found a so-called "Fender Duck" of great interest. This latter decoy had a very flat wooden body weighted by sheet lead on the bottom. No one knew much about it, but apparently it antedated by many years the cast-iron deck decoys or wing ducks, used on the modern battery.

Together with three Ruddies, still in fair condition, these additional finds traveled north with me on a Cape Charles sleeper—the gift of my host. They will never go overboard again; nor hear the roar of guns overhead. Scarred and faded but still intrepid, they were off to see the world in a knobby burlap bag—to use the familiar term—"collected."

Under similar circumstances and over a period of years, I have examined thousands of decoys. Localities change and personnel, but the other things remain constant. On southern landing or north Atlantic lighthouse, the waterfront is always there—and its followers, the Lee Dudleys and the Paxton Ewells.

Of recent years, decoys have found their way to antique shops but I prefer the adventure of finding my own. All those who have enjoyed the pleasure and thrills of duck shooting will smile at this. I smile myself, but of all birds subject to attraction by decoys, I am perhaps, the most susceptible bird of all.

Approximately two hundred have been assembled for historical reference. Only twenty are required to cover the range of decoyable ducks and geese, with another ten or twelve to show female painting patterns. Beyond this point, however, many examples are necessary to cover characteristics developed by locality and conditions under which the lures are used. Shore bird decoys are represented by a large group from different sections of the coast. Here again actual species are limited, but to represent the work of the past many examples are required.

But collecting old decoys offers an interesting field. They have been made and used for over a hundred years and can still be found on the original ground. Among the old hand makers, there were no standards other than those imposed by utility and competition. The product varied with the individual like handwriting. Range of type, therefore, is unlimited, offering many features of interest to the student of wild fowling.

There is also a vision of the perfect decoy; always before one, but constantly elusive. I, for one, have come to believe there is no such thing. Decoys are used under varied conditions and comparison is difficult. In their own particular place many decoys have unquestioned superiority, but a superiority limited to locality or purpose. As one becomes familiar with the picture as a whole, no single wooden duck or snipe seems able to carry the burden of perfection.

My own collection has a singular if personal importance. To me it represents the history of American waterfowl, their rise and fall. Yet the origin and development of decoys has remained in persistent obscurity. No separate treatise on the subject has ever appeared, likewise no pictorial records of early examples. With these facts before me, I have collected old decoys and painted portraits of typical examples. My book is like an island, a single gesture in the midst of unrelated activities. No one has ever bothered about them as I have, perhaps no one ever thought about it. But it is my wish that the decoy ducks of American duck shooting have a pedigree of their own. For this reason I become collector and historian.

The Art of Decoy Making

. . . And I says, says I,
Take an ax, man, and be done with it.
But they must lie in a sea and ride
Like a hove-to Gloucester schooner.

PEOPLE have different ideas about decoys. There are those who believe that "anything will do," and perhaps they are right. Most of us have killed ducks over very cock-eyed rigs. But there are others more particular—little known men of a special discrimination who raised the American decoy to the level of a homely classic.

The decoy was the answer to early America's demand for waterfowl, a permanent, heavy-duty lure. It grew up in remote localities and the whole process of development took place in shanty workshops. But the idea was "strong medicine." For over a hundred years it has been in constant operation and is still without dishonor.

By whom, or on what sylvan shore the first one was made, can never be known; or on what virgin water it lay at anchor. But the ripple of its launching has never ceased to widen. The idea was sound, destined to found and outlive the greatest era of wild fowl shooting the world has ever known.

Little can be learned of the men who developed the trade of "stool maker." Duck shooting came and roared its noisy way;

[8]

PLATE 2
RUDDY DUCKS *by Lee Dudley*
Knotts Island, Virginia

PLATE 3
CANVAS-BACK AND REDHEAD HEADS, NORMAL AND OVERSIZE
Knotts Island, Virginia

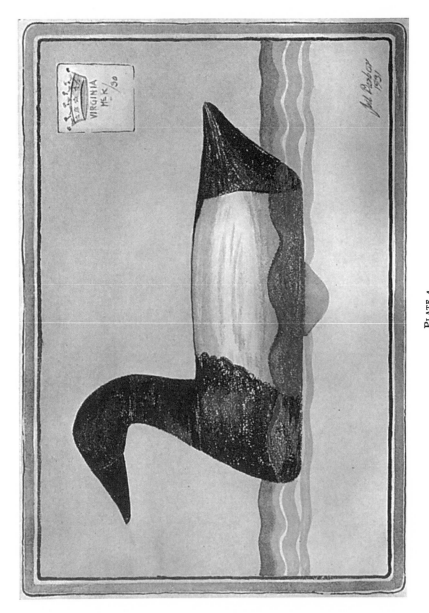

PLATE 4
OVERSIZE CANVAS-BACK
Knotts Island, Virginia

America dined on Canvas-back, Redhead, Ruddy Duck and Black Duck. We killed a legacy of waterfowl over decoys but the decoy maker stayed consistently behind the scenes—always over the horizon. He was one enemy the birds could never understand.

One presumes that the early makers worked on the original basis that—"anything would do." It is well known they were notoriously underpaid. Many of them failed or refused to follow more lucrative pursuits but somehow, and it is difficult to specify just how, the decoy maker has become a figure in American history. In the hands of these little known men, the fashioning of decoys grew into an off-season trade. At prices ranging from twenty to fifty cents apiece, its followers evolved a sculpture all their own. Pressed for time and money, they made not ducks at all, but what is more important, a symbolism that portrays our vanishing waterfowl.

Their accomplishment has something queer about it, and to my mind it was quite unconsciously arrived at. One may call it art, an art that came unasked, but can never be duplicated. The conditions which produced it are in limbo, solitudes broken, lanes of migration shrunken, and wild ducks under the protection of the Federal Government. But in spite of increasing restrictions, the decoy survives, unchanged and unbeaten, but moving onward into the world of souvenir.

The present interest in decoys had its beginning in a shortage which developed right after the World War. With the passing of market gunning in 1918, production abruptly ceased. Due to conditions at this period, decoy makers and decoy factories went suddenly out of business. The situation righted itself after a few seasons and the incident forgotten; meanwhile, a new era dawned. Following the War, and due to necessity, the sportsman at large became his own decoy maker.

That post-war and amateur activity held many surprises. What seemed so simple, presented difficulties too numerous and subtle to catalogue. In most instances, and due to lack of real knowledge, the tyro tried to copy old work. But forgery, even by good mechanics, proved elusive and success was rare. Attempts at improvement went queerly amiss; even the plumage patterns established by shanty naturalists resisted the unaccustomed hands. Altogether the making of decoys by amateurs proved a unique and baffling experience. It resulted, however, in a new and deep respect for the men of the past.

As a result of this adventure, decoys came out of their shell. Evidence of this was shown by a "Decoy Show," held in Bellport, L. I., in the summer of 1923. Whimsical as it seemed, the following year saw a second show in the City of New York. After this event interest subsided, to revive again in an "Exhibition of Wild Fowl Decoys," held in New York in the fall of 1931.

All three of these exhibitions were conducted by and in the interest of sportsmen. The underlying purpose was to discover if possible the secrets of a simple old trade. "Old Decoys" while a feature of these shows, were regarded in the light of curios; their salient qualities still unrecognized. However, this effort on the part of sportsmen represents the first step toward the recognition of qualities in decoys other than of utility.

The next move lay quite outside of sporting circles. In November of 1931 the Newark Museum sponsored an exhibition of so-called American Folk Sculpture and included among the exhibits a group of old decoys. Here, in company of cigar store Indians, figure heads of sailing ships and other examples of early American craftsmanship, decoy ducks took over the title of "Primitive Polychrome Sculpture."

For the first time in the history of art stool ducks were catalogued: "Canvas-back from the Chesapeake," "Barnegat Canada Goose," "Black Duck from the Great South Bay," and many others. Strange names to the new world of art. To some of us it was gratifying, the more so as the introduction to the catalogue carried the following observation:

"Wild fowl decoys constitute a most extensive field for the

PLATE 5
OLD ROCKING HORSE
Stratford, Conn.

PLATE 6
PINTAIL DRAKE *by John Blair*
Delaware Bay, 1865

PLATE 7

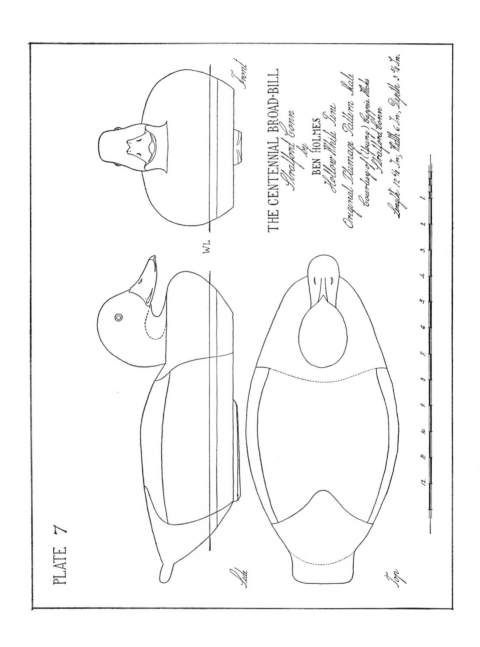

THE CENTENNIAL BROAD-BILL
Stratford Conn.
by
BEN HOLMES
Hollow White Pine

Original Plumage Pattern Male
Courtesy of (Young) Bayne Abel
Stratford Conn.

Length 12¼ in., Width 6 in., Depth 3¾ in.

collector, and they have a special appeal for lovers of Americana."

"Americana!" That indeed is the word to classify the decoys of American duck shooting. . . . They are truly a fragment of history. Every old fireside in America felt the influence of wild ducks. By accident of economics their gift to mankind is commemorated in the hatchet sculpture of the decoy maker, the man who gave no thought to it but accomplished art—the only art our wild life left behind.

AMERICANA

"Americana," the catalogue runs
And down below. . . .
"Canvas-back decoy from Maryland."
And here I am, on a museum shelf
Watching dust rise and settle again
On faded curios.

Americana! And I had rather lie
At anchor off Havre de Grace
Or drift to leeward, derelict
And spend my days
Stored somewhere on the Eastern Shore
In a shanty.

Americana? Why spent shot
Is better off than I
On the bottom of the Chesapeake
And that's where I would rather be,
Water-logged and bound in tendrils
Of wild celery.

Americana? No! But lying there,
Shadows would pass above,
Wild Geese and Canvas-back,
Phantom boats and men,
And now and then, the white breasts
Of rafting Swan.

J. B.

PART II

PLATE 8
REDHEAD WITH FLAPPING WINGS *by Capt. Charlie Do Ville*
Lake Ontario, about 1880

PLATE 9
OLD CORK BLACK DUCK
Shinnecock Bay, L. I.

PLATE 10

BUSHWHACKING DUCKS ON THE CHESAPEAKE

From a Swan Boat

"Bushwhacking simply means sculling toward a paddling of ducks in a boat that has a screen around it high enough to conceal the fowler and the man at the oar; or in a craft which resembles a huge swan, and is accompanied by decoys, which are placed on each side. The latter is only large enough to contain two men, and one of these shoots while the other uses the oar through an aperture in the rear part of the mock swan, to prevent it from being seen by the birds." From "American Game Shooting," by John Mortimer Murphy, 1882.

III

Wild Duck Shooting

Pursuit of wild fowl in America is a natural. As there was no husbandry or organized food supply, the colonist turned naturally to sources at hand—one of them wild fowl.

Although few records are available the early picture is fairly clear. Due to climatic and food conditions vast numbers of ducks and geese found winter feeding grounds on the bays and estuaries of the Atlantic Coast. These concentration areas included certain warm spots on the upper coast but the most significant grounds began at the Great South Bay in the vicinity of New York and extended southward through Barnegat, the Chesapeake, and the land-locked coastal waters of Virginia and the Carolinas. The other important ground with respect to what followed lay along the Gulf of Mexico.

This geographical condition brought waterfowl in close proximity to coastal settlements along the whole seaboard from Louisiana north to New England. It made a perfect set-up— millions of edible birds seasonably at the very door of the new and undeveloped country.

Practical use of this bird life was inevitable, and actually began with explorers. The conditions which confronted the participants were quite different from those existing in the older countries and a new principle was arrived at—one based on Indian devices. Although later carried back to Europe this method is purely and wholly American.

WILD FOWL DECOYS

In outlining this procedure, my concern is chiefly with the method of gunning wild ducks, geese and shore birds which share a distinctive characteristic—susceptibility to attraction by decoys. It is the application of this fact which has served throughout the long history of our wild fowling.

While not quite accurate to refer to this activity as duck shooting, I will do so. Shore bird shooting, while conducted along similar lines, has less economic importance and will have its own chapter. What follows also has mostly to do with coastal gunning, as it was here that the custom had its origin and greatest development.

Decoys, as we know them now, did not appear at once. In the beginning birds were secured in various ways. Stories are still current along the Chesapeake of ducks taken in gill nets suspended below the surface of the water; but gunning predominated. The netting devices of Europe, based on requirements of older and larger communities, were cumbersome and unnecessary. The American who had acquired the gun habit by force of circumstances, preferred to use guns anyway—and did so. His steady use of gunpowder was also coincident with and had much to do with the rapid development of firearms of the period.

The gunners were of three types. In every locality was the occasional gunner who shot ducks for food only. On the upper coast his activities were confined largely to the spring and fall flights, although the thrifty Yankee has always made a practice of killing sea ducks which remain off his coast all winter.

The next duck shooter to appear was the sportsman, an enviable and serene figure of the 'fifties. It is through him and his literary efforts that we obtain our first records of duck shooting as an art; also our first glimpse of that ghostly figure in American shooting called the Market Gunner.

The conditions which produced this third type of duck shooter could only have happened in a free-for-all country like ours. He came into the picture through the rapid growth of population coupled with a growing demand for wild ducks. How well he supplied this demand is now a matter of national regret. In his hands the practice of killing for individual or family use developed rapidly to a profession of ducking on a large scale for commercial distribution, and was followed by experts, experts in the strictest sense of the word.

Market shooting, like many other and similar activities, had its beginning on the coast, but as the country spread westward professional gunning followed, reaching a point of extravagance amounting to savagery. The fact remains, however, American ducking, as developed by these little known men, will stand for all time as the greatest era of wild fowl shooting the world has ever known.

And the market gunner, more than any other, is the father of decoys. This important innovation came into prominence during the expansion of economic gunning which took place just before the middle of the 19th century. It came in the form of a crude floating duck, hewn out of wood and designed for hard usage. Formed roughly to simulate various species of ducks, geese and brant, to be known later by the name of decoy, it became the determining factor in all subsequent wild fowl shooting in America.

IV

Market Gunning

In the year 1918, the American market gunner folded his weatherbeaten equipment and passed quietly out of the picture; he was through. He left no records. His activities, while not unlawful, lay close to an undercurrent of public disfavor. He kept his mouth shut, confining results to dealers and private account books. During the 'eighties, feeling against over-shooting ran so high that many private ducking clubs kept their totals from the public. Even at that time it was one thing to dine royally on Canvas-back, but quite another to contemplate the professional, his heavy guns, unlimited ammunition, and business of killing wild ducks for the market.

As the episode recedes, however, criticism is tempered with understanding and details of what is now a fading episode become of value.

While published records are scarce, references do occur, principally in books on wild fowling, indicating the extent to which gunning was carried on. One of the earliest of these occurs in Krider's *Sporting Anecdotes,* published in the year 1853.* In a chapter telling of duck shooting on the Chesapeake, he refers to a Havre de Grace gunner who "killed one hundred and sixty-three Canvas-backs on the tenth day of December last" ... also "that in the spring of 1850 the same famous duck

*John Krider, Krider's "Sporting Anecdotes." A. Hart, late Cary and Hart, Philadelphia, 1853.

shooter killed two hundred and seventy Canvas-backs and Redheads." Later in the same chapter he remarks that "several thousand ducks were brought into the town that day (Havre de Grace) by the different parties shooting on the Flats."

A similar reference occurs in *The American Sportsman**
published a few years later. Again, in a chapter devoted to battery shooting over decoys on the Chesapeake, the author names a well-known local gunner who killed as many as one hundred and eighty-seven Canvas-backs in one day, and "during the seasons of 1846–1847 actually bagged seven thousand Canvas-backs."

After the middle of the century, little information with respect to commercial gunning was given out. So, to continue the record, I resort to story telling. While somewhat legendary, the accounts come from local sources and are correct in essentials. One of these has to do with market gunning on the Great South Bay, as related by Captain Wilbur A. Corwin, expert bayman and gunner, with a flair for historical events. It tells of a big day on the bay, in his father's time.

During the season of 1898, the story goes, Captain Corwin, Sr., was operating a gunning rig on the Great South Bay off Bellport. The rig consisted of a double battery with a set of about two hundred and fifty decoys. The crew was made up of Captain Corwin, a second gun, and a man to tend.

On this particular occasion the battery was moored off the old coast guard station on the ocean beach near Fiddleton Point. The season was late December and conditions perfect, with swarms of birds in motion. The members of the crew were experts and spelled each other to keep two men constantly in the box. Shooting began at daylight and continued steadily all day.

The story of what transpired contains enough material to complete an essay on the art of battery shooting, but that I leave in the hands of others, and proceed with figures. Before night-

*Elisha J. Lewis, "The American Sportsman." Published at Philadelphia, 1855.

fall the crew had shot and picked up the astounding number
of six hundred and forty birds, mostly Broadbill. At the prevailing rate of 25c. a pair, this one day's shoot netted Captain
Corwin in the neighborhood of $65.00, F.O.B. Bellport.

On visits to the Chesapeake, I have listened to reminiscences
concerning many men and events. I have traveled from North
East and Elkton, Maryland, down the Eastern Shore to Cape
Charles, but nowhere in that paradise of waterfowl is there a
story of duck shooting equal to that told of William Dobson of
Havre de Grace. Stories of this extraordinary man are still
current among older residents of the village, but one event is
outstanding. Although previously reviewed by my friend,
George Hopper, it bears repetition.*

Dobson, it appears, was something of an autocrat, one
who took no part in handling boats or gear. He was battery
gunner only. When the time came for him to do his stuff, he
went aboard the box with guns and shells, his sole duty being to
kill on-coming birds. Socially, he is reported to have been shy
and an indifferent shot at local trap shoots. Alone in a battery,
however, he is acknowledged to have been the fastest and most
accurate shooting man the Chesapeake ever produced.

Some years ago, while talking with Captain W. E. Moore
of Havre de Grace about old-time gunning, Dobson's name
was mentioned. Upon inquiry it appeared that he and Captain
Moore had been friends and rival gunners from boyhood. And
there in an old Havre de Grace parlor, I heard again the story
of the "five hundred Redhead." For the purpose of record I
give the essential details.

" 'It happened right here, on the flats off Havre de Grace,'
verified Capt. Moore, 'on the opening day of the season in 1879.
On that one day, Dobson killed over five hundred ducks—
there is no question about it. He started out as usual shooting
two guns, double breech loaders of ten guage. During the early
hours of the morning, one gun burst and was thrown overboard.

*"Canvas-back Shooting," by George F. Hopper.

Birds were coming in so steadily there was no time to replace it. He continued shooting all day with the remaining gun, keeping it cool by frequent immersion in the bay. When results were tallied that evening, it was found that Mr. Dobson had shot five hundred and nine birds. About sixty Canvas-backs, the remainder Redheads.' "

Captain Moore was in his eighty-seventh year when this story was told, and had spent the working years of his life on the bay. As a young man he prowled the Susquehanna Flats at night, paddling one of the notorious Big Guns, but in the 'seventies went over to batteries. During this period he lost his lower right arm in a "gun accident," but his ability to shoot was unimpaired and he went back to the Bay. In later years he captained the gunning yacht "Reckless" owned by Mr. William Polhemus of New York. The "Reckless," a Chesapeake scow of fabulous appointments together with the gunning rig was left as a legacy to her skipper at the death of the owner. The Captain himself passed out of the picture some years ago, he and his memories of big guns, batteries, sportsmen and ducks.

These records of battery shooting show results accomplished by crews of three and in some cases four men. I will give one more incident therefore, showing the work of a single individual as related by Captain Jesse Birdsall of Barnegat Village, N. J. The methods of Barnegat Bay differ from those of Long Island, the Chesapeake, and southern waters, because the battery or sink-box has never been permitted. For the most part the gunning here is conducted in a small boat of local design called a "sneak-box," and operated by one or at most two men. In pre-power boat days the baymen rowed to and from the gunning ground, the boat loaded with passenger-sportsmen, guns, ammunition, and from thirty to forty-two decoys.

To reduce weight of equipment, Barnegat decoys, therefore, are specially constructed. Bodies are made in two sections to permit of being hollowed out—locally designated as "dug-outs." In talking of this feature with Captain Birdsall, he some-how veered off to the subject of a certain muzzle loader shot-gun for which he seemed to hold a great affection. The size of the gun was not mentioned but I inferred that it was a sup-posedly retired and, at that time, illegal Eight. The Captain was a celebrated gunner of the old school, and the end of the story carried an item of interest.

"In the winter of 1899," the story ran, "I killed one hundred and fifteen birds with that gun, in one day's shooting. Yes sir— one hundred and fifteen, not counting cripples!" And he added: "It took just exactly one pound of powder; the powder ran out or I'd got more."

This conversation occurred during the winter of 1922. The Captain at that time was seventy years old, but still followed the bay. The story, of course, carried irrelevant details, but on the day mentioned he alone had shot and picked up the birds, Broadbill and Redhead, and rowed them home.

So much for professional gunning on winter feeding grounds of the middle Atlantic coast. Here, and also on the shores of New England, the economic use of waterfowl de-veloped into a serious problem. The conditions which brought about its close are well known. It appears that over and above American extravagance, lies a deep affection for wild fowl. The first step toward their conservation dates way back to an Act passed by the State of Rhode Island in 1846. From that time on conservation forces steadily increased, finally achieving country-wide prohibition against Spring shooting, shooting at night, and the shipment of birds. These restrictions were issued under the Federal Migratory Bird Law in the year 1913. A few years later the sale of game was brought to an end by the Migratory Bird Treaty Act of July 3, 1918. Under the provisions of this Law, this country entered into an agreement with Canada which protected the waterfowl of North Amer-ica over the entire range of migratory flight.

PLATE 11
CANVAS-BACK *by Capt. Ben Dye*
Havre de Grace, Md., 1880

PLATE 12
OLD CANVAS-BACK WING-DUCK
Elkton, Md.

PLATE 13
MALE SHELDRAKE *by Henry F. Osborn*
Bellport, L. I., 1846

PLATE 14
BATTERY SHOOTING ON THE GREAT SOUTH BAY *by Arthur Schneider*

MARKET GUNNING

The effect of these regulations was far-reaching. The economic use of wild fowl, which had endured for over a century, came to an end, marking the close of an historic period. Prohibition against the sale of game, made gunning for the market unlawful and American duck shooting became the highly restricted sport we now enjoy, short open seasons and limited bags.

I seem to have digressed, perhaps said too much about the professional gunner. His need, however, of permanent heavy duty lures to be used in the solitudes of deep and wide waters, was the greatest factor in the development of the American system. Not all, of course, but by far the greater part of his birds were lured to ambush and killed over decoys. In the history of American wild fowling, the professional gunner and decoys are inseparable.

PART III

PLATE 15

FEMALE BROADBILL *by Capt. Cooper Predmore*
Barnegat Village, N. J., about 1880

PLATE 16

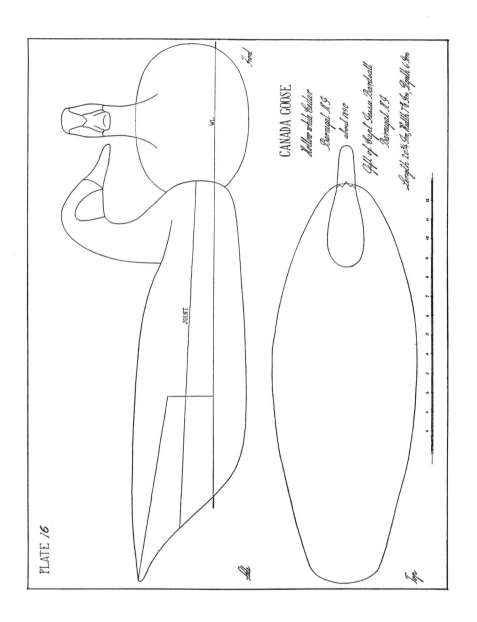

CANADA GOOSE

Yellow with Cedar
Barnegat N J
about 1890

Aft of Capt Jesse Randall
Barnegat N J

Length 20½ In, Width 7⅝ In, Depth 6 In.

V

Old Country Decoys

THE WORD "DECOY" has special and ancient significance with reference to fowling. It may be defined as a lure—something to mislead and entice the unsuspecting. In original signification, however, a decoy is a place or pond provided with an arrangement for the capture of waterfowl. According to Sir Ralph Payne-Gallwey,* the present form of the word is a contraction of the Dutch expression—"ENDE-KOOY"—meaning duck-cage, or trap.

Invention of the duck-cage is attributed to Holland and antedates the general use of firearms. In the early years of fowling, both the cage and method of capture were primitive. A pond or bay frequented by waterfowl would be fenced with nets, open at the leeward end and provided with "V" shaped enclosures or cages at the windward end. When birds in sufficient numbers had assembled within the confined area, they were driven down the net barriers by men in boats to the cages from which they were later taken and dispatched. Accounts of driving waterfowl indicate that the process took place during the summer months and the birds so taken are described as "young or moulting."

In course of time the process of driving birds was abandoned in favor of a more effective one. The simple palisade was developed into an arrangement of net-covered canals or pipes,

*Sir Ralph Payne-Gallwey, Bart. "The Book of Duck Decoys," London, 1886.

radiating from a central enclosed pond. These "pipes" extended off into the marsh, changing direction at intervals to eliminate long vistas. Each pipe terminated in a removable tunnel-net in which the birds were entrapped.

Operation of the improved device followed a different procedure. The assembled birds were no longer driven, but *enticed*

PLATE 17
DRIVING WILD FOWL, 16TH CENTURY
From an old print

into the mouth of the pipes. To accomplish this the men operating the decoy employed a trained dog assisted by semi-domesticated wild ducks. The birds so employed were called "Coy Ducks." It was the duty of the trained birds to lure strangers into the mouth of the pipe, after which they were urged on to the trammel nets. The lures, being unafraid, returned to the pond unharmed. These cheaters directed by the unseen Coyman are the original decoy ducks.

It is recorded that in the year 1665 King Charles of Eng-

PLATE 18
DUCK DECOY PIPE
From "The Wild-Fowler," by Folkard, 1875

PLATE 19
TUNNEL NET
From "The Wild-Fowler," by Folkard, 1875

PLATE 20

HUT SHOOTING ON THE FRENCH SYSTEM

From Col. Hawker, "Instructions to Young Sportsmen"

land imported a famous Coy-man from Holland, and established the first of a long line of decoys in the British Isles. At that time the extensive fens of the Eastern counties provided feeding and breeding grounds for vast numbers of waterfowl. Firearms of the period were too imperfect to be effective on a large scale and the imported device developed rapidly. Ultimately these duck decoys supplied the English with an abundance of wild fowl.

It is of interest to know that in out-of-the-way corners of England, duck decoys are still in operation. J. Whitaker, writing in 1918 reports 28 decoys now being worked in the British Isles.*

From this outline of Dutch and English fowling, it will be seen that the original decoy was a "Duck-cage" or netting device. It is uncertain whether the contracted form of decoy is of English or Dutch extraction, but at first signified a trap in which wild ducks were captured alive. Investigation may be summed up by saying that the one-time duck-cage became a "decoy," and the live "coy-duck" used as a lure was the original decoy duck.

Study of English methods indicates slight acquaintance with artificial decoys. One exception, however, is the so-called "Stale," or birdskin crudely stuffed with straw. The stale is employed in the taking of Plover and set up on sand bars as in America. In the process, however, the birds are not shot as in America, but captured in nets.

Nowadays wooden decoy ducks are available in England and receive occasional notice in modern works on wild fowl shooting. Some years ago a firm of Bristol gun-makers sent me a Decoy Wood Pigeon, made of wood and painted as to color, but I am unfamiliar with its use. It is well known, however, that artificial lures have never been adopted by British fowlers, a fact commented on as recently as 1926. Mr. J. M. C. Nichols, in his *Birds of Marsh and Mere,* remarks: "The use of

*J. Whitaker, "British Duck Decoys of Today," London, 1918.

decoys (artificial birds) for any form of wild fowl shooting is a method very little practiced in any part of England, but is much used abroad, in Canada, the U. S. A. and elsewhere."

During the latter part of the 18th century, the development of firearms brought about a new use for decoy ducks. In the new procedure, instead of luring waterfowl to nets, trained live birds were employed to attract them within range of weapons.

Apparently the practice had its origin in France, and is designated *La Chasse à la Hutte*. Here the live decoy birds are given the name of *Appelants* (Callers). Col. Hawker, in the early part of the 19th century, describes the sport as follows:

". . . The waters here are rented by different 'huttiers' (hut-shooters)—who get the chief of their living by supplying the markets of Paris and other towns—with wild fowl, which they shoot, instead of taking them by decoys (nets), as in our country.

". . . This hut being built among the high reeds, and afterwards strewed over with them, is completely invisible; although as commodious inside as a large covered cart. Here the huttier of Perone goes regularly every night, wet or dry, and takes a great coat (if he has one), with a piece of brown bread, and a sour apple for his supper. In front of his hut are fastened, two piles at each end, three separate ropes, about twenty yards long. On the center one, he ties four drakes and to the one on each flank, four ducks; making in all twelve decoy birds; and these being (to use a military term) dressed in line, whatever bird he sees out of ranks he knows must be a wild one; and as the lake, in moderate weather, is like a mirror, the night is seldom so dark but that he can see to shoot at the very short distance which his miserable gun, and miserable powder, will kill."*

*Lt. Col. P. Hawker, "Instructions to Young Sportsmen." Fifth edition, London, 1826.

PLATE 21
MALE EUROPEAN TEAL
Paris, France, 1900

PLATE 22
FEMALE EUROPEAN TEAL
Paris, France, 1900

EUROPEAN WIDGEON   PLATE 23   SCAUP
CONTEMPORARY FRENCH DECOYS

PLATE 24
MODERN GERMAN DECOY

It will be remarked that Col. Hawker's account of live decoys was published in the year 1826. In thorough-going British fashion he appears to cover all contemporary features. Presumably the artificial caller had not yet put in appearance.

About fifty years later another English writer makes note of artificial birds then used by French fowlers. The reference is brief, merely stating, "A few skins of ducks, stuffed with straw, are often interspersed with the live fowl (callers) when the huttier's decoy ducks are few in number."*

No record as to the introduction of wooden decoys in France is available, but at this time they are employed as in America although to much more limited extent. They are utilized for night shooting, also during the day on ponds and marshes, but mostly in company with live callers. The preferred material, wood, is indicated by the name *Appelant en Bois* (calling in wood).

The common decoys used in night shooting are painted black. Those used during daylight hours are finished in colors. Plover and other shore bird shooting is conducted over complete sets of wooden decoys as in America. This form of wildfowl shooting is termed *La Chasse aux Appelants*.

In general fashion the French decoy follows American lines, similar, yet distinctly foreign. The pair of European Teal pictured in Plates Nos. 21 and 22, show typical French decoys of something over thirty years ago. They were purchased in Paris by Dr. John C. Phillips of Boston, in 1900. The decoy shown in Plate No. 23 gives the all-black example employed in night shooting only.

Study of contemporary French authorities, however, indicate that the wooden decoy has never been developed as in America, a conclusion borne out by Ternier in his *Les Canards Sauvages*. In the chapter of this volume devoted to *les Appelants,* he makes this observation with respect to wooden callers, or in his nomenclature—the *Blette*.

*H. C. Folkard, "The Wild-Fowler," London, 1875.

". . . The name 'Blette,' given here to ducks made of wood, zinc, cork or to stuffed birds, is generally used to designate them. . . . Indeed, I consider the *Blettes* better than a display of undisciplined or bad singing callers, but the *Blette* cannot be used as substitute for good callers, and by comparison, their presence can prove detrimental to the game, as most of the *Blettes* that I have seen resemble very vaguely live ducks and were, in most instances, covered with extravagant *peinturlurge*."

Less seriously, M. Ternier also remarks: "A *Blette* which goes back to its frame at every ripple of water has no 'IT' and cannot tempt a flying bird looking for company." The chapter concludes in masterly fashion thus: ". . . that all such equipment (decoys) should be stable, dull and quiet. At all times they must be passed practically unnoticed, and that this effaced rôle is the only one that becomes them."*

In the author's opinion this is good advice, not only for France but for any other country.

One who sets out to acquire history, accumulates odds and ends of information difficult to substantiate. This kind of data seems carried in air like pollen—potent but often elusive. I have long been aware of this source and sometimes profit, but not always.

For example, I meet a small dark woman at a party. With pronounced accent she remarks on the attractiveness of the room. I agree in particular with respect to an Audubon print

* Data on the subject of modern French decoys was acquired through the courtesy of M. Paul Ullern of Paris. At the close of a letter received in February, 1932, he remarks that "All sorts of material is employed in the making of French decoys, even old wooden shoes are frequently enlisted." Rather an interesting idea.

Translation, Ternier & Masse, "Les Canards Sauvages et Leurs Congénères," Paris, France, 1907.

on the wall. The lady likewise admires. Then, after the fashion of collectors, I divert the conversation to my own and favorite subject. I am good at this, very good.

The lady, an Italian countess, is led to tell of a Villa where many times she had been a guest. It was an old Villa, south of Florence, with gardens extending to the shore of a lake. The picture was very clear. At the foot of the garden stood a ruined belvedere, and below, near the water edge, a hut.

Park Avenue, a villa, a countess. Pollen in the air. In the hut, of course, were wooden ducks, "painted mostly in blue and white," and old, very old. On occasion one or two of them occupied a fountain on the upper terrace, but that was all. Long after, a letter from the countess informed me that the villa was in other hands. "The war had changed everything." The wooden ducks from Italy never came.

An artist friend leans back in his chair and behind a screen of cigarette smoke remarks: "Why the Chinese had perfectly swell decoy ducks. I have seen them in old prints." Some day perhaps I will come across that antique Chinese print. I am enough historian, to firmly believe I will.

But not all pollen is lost. Another friend tells of an allusion to decoy ducks "before Christ himself." Not quite correct, but the reference clicks. In a fascinating volume called *Sport in Classic Times,** I find a chapter on ancient fowling. After poring through items concerning horse-hair noose, fowling rods, throwing sticks, even ancient poetry on fowling, the classic decoy appears. The passage refers to the methods of ancient Greece. I quote:

"One way of hunting them (ducks) was by torch light, when boats were probably pushed through the reeds and the ducks driven into nets; and a similar way of hunting sea-birds by night is recorded in Ixeutia. The other way was by wooden decoys, shaped and painted after nature, and held by a long

*"Sport in Classic Times," by A. J. Butler, D. Litt. Fellow of Brasenose College, Oxford. Fellow of Eton College.

string. Here the hunter was hidden, and slowly towing his decoy, drew the duck either within range for sticks and missiles or probably led them into a tunnel of netting, such as is well known in England today. This conjecture is confirmed by another passage in the Ixeutia, which definitely tells of wild-geese lured by a wooden decoy into a channel where a net suddenly closes upon them. These painted wooden decoys furnish strange examples of the nearness of the ancient to the modern world. A more original device, which has not become traditional, was the use of a painted picture as a decoy for the sea-birds called Plungers—perhaps Skua Gulls. The picture showing a brightly colored fish was painted on a hard panel and anchored afloat, and the Plunger diving swiftly from a height upon it, broke his neck."

Can you beat that?

The countries of the Scandinavian Peninsula offer more recent and definite information. The waters of Sweden and Denmark attract vast numbers of waterfowl and have been the scene of extensive fowling for centuries. Methods employed range from the primitive horse-hair noose to the stalking horse and a hazardous pursuit termed "rock-fowling." The duck decoy as identified with Holland and the British Isles is unknown but the ancient Fogel-Nat (fowling net) plays a similar and effective part.

L. Lloyd, in his volume on Scandinavian fowling* describes these customs at length, among them a method similar to our own. The passage is brief but illuminating. I will quote Mr. Lloyd:

"Another plan of shooting waterfowl in the Gottenborg and others of the Scandinavian Skargardar is by the aid of the so-called *Wettar,* or artificial decoy birds. These consist either of such as are stuffed, or of blocks of wood so fashioned and painted as to resemble live waterfowl. The fowler anchors his *Wettar* by means of pieces of string and small stones, within

*L. Lloyd, "Game Birds and Wild Fowl of Sweden and Norway," London, 1867.

easy gunshot of some headland the fowl are in the habit of passing in their morning and evening flights."

As to the introduction of such decoys in Scandinavia, no dates are available. It is of interest, however, to note that in November of 1931, Sweden and Norway entered into a treaty under the terms of which the *Wettar* is now prohibited.

Ultimately I expect to add decoys from Sweden and Norway to my collection, and, from what I know of these maritime nations, expectation runs high. I even visualize them, lying at anchor off some rugged headland, ultra seaworthy like deep-water ships. I even anticipate stone anchors made fast in fastidious nautical fashion.

There remains Germany of which my knowledge of decoys is hearsay only. I show a German decoy, however, discovered in a boat-house on the south shore of Long Island. At the time, I was visiting a New York sportsman for the purpose of inspecting a group of splendid old shore-bird decoys of which more is to follow.

From my point of view the visit was a great success. On my return to New York the German Mallard came along, a gift from my smiling host. I could not resist the accompanying portrait.

VI

American Indian Bird Lures

As THE STORY of fowling arrives on American waters, conditions and methods undergo a distinct change. It has been noted that long prior to the general use of firearms, Europeans employed live birds to entice wild waterfowl to capture by nets; later to within range of fowling pieces. It is also a fact that artificial birds in connection with old world fowling, do not appear in published records until after the middle of the 19th century.

But in primitive America the taming or domestication of animals or fowl was unknown. Communities as in Europe did not exist and the use of natural fowl was confined to individual or family. This difference in conditions has a definite bearing on the adoption of the American system.

The prevailing method employed by the native Indian was definitely to lure wild ducks within range of primitive weapons by the use of dead, improvised or wholly artificial birds.

With our knowledge of surviving customs, together with ancient remains, the evolution of these devices may be clearly seen. The most primitive were obtained by mud-heaps, built up in shoal water, roughly simulating a group of birds on the surface. Equally crude, were bunches of dried grass supported on sticks. Another early artifice, and a favorite one, was the employment of dead birds. In shoal water the birds so used were maintained in position by a crotched stick thrust in the bottom, or by a long reed inserted in the throat of the fowl, broken at the neck to bring the head down, the large end then being secured to the bottom as a mooring. On deep water, dead birds rode at anchor, several on a line. In this instance heads hung down in semblance of live fowl feeding.

After these more or less temporary figures comes the effort toward a permanent utensil. The first of these consisted of mounted duck heads for use on shore. Later, bird skins stuffed with dried grass and mounted on floats were developed for use on deep water. Finally the wholly artificial bird appeared, ancient examples of which are a matter of record.

Perfect examples of these aboriginal decoys were discovered by scientists while excavating for evidence of ancient Indian culture in southwestern United States.* The decoys were found in company with other objects in the Lovelock Cave of Nevada and attributed to a vanished civilization called "Tule Eaters," predecessors of the Northern Paiutes. The bird lures, protected by a basket-like container, were located about four feet below the floor of the cave, buried beneath an accumulation of ages. Due to climatic conditions similar to those of Egypt and Peru, the specimens were in a perfect state of preservation.

The Lovelock decoys are of two kinds—stuffed or mounted skins and complete artificial birds made of tule.† The first type consisted of heads, Canada Geese, Sheldrake and other species mounted on rush forms. The wholly artificial birds were represented by Canvas-backs of most ingenious construction. (See Plate No. 27.)

*See "Excavations of the Lovelock Cave, 1911–1924." Llewellyn L. Loud and M. R. Harrington, University of California Press, 1929.
  The Lovelock Cave is located in the Humbolt Range of mountains, near the little town of Lovelock, Nevada. Excavation was conducted for The Museum of the American Indian, Hey Foundation, of New York, by Mr. A. Raymond Harrington in 1924. Through the courtesy of Mr. Harrington, permission was obtained to illustrate one of the eleven decoys discovered.

†Tule, a large variety of the common great bull-rush found in marshes and lakes in western United States.

WILD FOWL DECOYS

In this latter type the body of the decoy is formed by bending a bundle of bull-rush stems and binding together with twisted strands of the same material. The head, likewise formed of rushes, is secured to the body in such a manner as to obtain a most lifelike pose. At the end, the rushes are cut to simulate the duck's tail. The forward part is smoothly bound to give the swell of breast. The white belt of the male Canvas-back is accomplished by the introduction of feathers. The portrait is completed by native paints—head, breast and tail in brownish red or black as required by the natural plumage. Scientific authorities fail to establish the exact date of these decoys, designating them as pre-Caucasian and belonging to the "Later Period," an era having its beginning about the year A.D. 1000. Less conservative students, however, estimate their age as being nearer two thousand years.

Although we have no actual evidence, it is probable that superior workmanship of this kind was not confined to the natives of the Southwest. In fact a French explorer in the year 1687 records the use of stuffed bird skins on Lake Champlain —two thousand miles distant from the home of the "tule eaters." This precious evidence has two angles of interest. It shows the white man's early acquaintance with native methods, also the Indian procedure of over two hundred years ago. Actual data on early American wild fowling is so very rare, I quote the Baron Lahontan at length.*

"In the beginning of September, I set out in a canow upon several rivers, marshes and pools that disembogue in the Champlain Lake, being accompany'd with thirty or forty of the savages that are very expert in shooting and hunting, and perfectly well acquainted with the proper places for finding waterfowl, deer and other sallow beasts. The first spot we took up was upon the side of a marsh or fen, of four or five leagues in circumference: and after we had fitted up our huts,

*The Baron Lahontan, "New Voyages to North America." Original letter, Boucherville, May 28, 1687. Published, London, 1703. "Being a curious description of the hunting of divers animals."

PLATE 25
FISHING AND FOWLING, 6TH CENTURY, B.C.
From an Etruscan Tomb

PLATE 26
CALABASH DECOY OF INDIA
From "The Wild-Fowler," by Folkard, 1875

PLATE 27
PRE-WHITEMAN CANVAS-BACK
From Lovelock Cave, Nevada

PLATE 28
TULE CANVAS-BACK AND DECOY HEADS
From Lovelock Cave, Nevada

the savages made huts upon water in several places. These huts were made of the branches and leaves of trees and contained three or four men. For a decoy they have the skins of geese, bustards and ducks, dried and stuffed with hay. The two feet being made fast with two nails to a small piece of light plank, which float around the hut. The place being frequented by wonderfull numbers of geese, ducks, bustards, teals and an infinity of other waterfowls—see the stuffed skins swimming with their heads erected as if they were alive. They repair to the same place and so give the savages an opportunity of shooting them either flying or upon the water, after which the savages get into their canows and gather them up.

"They have likewise a way of catching them with nets, stretched upon the surface of the water at the entries of the rivers. In a word we eat nothing but waterfowl for fifteen days, after which we resolve to declare war against the Turtle Doves."

It must not be supposed that this listing of Indian devices represents a complete, continuous or progressive evolution. As custom or emergency dictates, primitive decoys are still employed. The Eskimos, Indians and White Men continue to use dead birds and modern Paiutes follow the ancient custom of mounting skins on tule forms. In the northwest, the incredible innocence of waterfowl is still demonstrated by the use of "mud heaps," to the tune of automatic shotguns.

In this age of vanishing Indian activities, I show, with great pleasure, a modern decoy from the Georgian Bay district of Canada. It is the work of Ojibway Indians. As shown in Plate No. 29, the illusion of a bird feeding is obtained by a silhouette supported on a body-like float. Both parts are made from the heavy bark of a tree called locally "cork elm." An impression of plumage is obtained by the application of real duck wings to the sides of the upright part.*

*The donor of these decoys, Mr. Ferd Luthy, Jr., of Peoria, Ill., informs me that the Ojibway Indians are very indifferent duck shooters and rarely employ decoys. As specimens of modern work, however, they are justly entitled to record.

WILD FOWL DECOYS

The "hunting grounds" of these decoys is a long way from Lake Champlain and of a craftsmanship more than two hundred years later. But the relation is still very close. The modern Indian on Georgian Bay employs a float to support his lure and feathers to accomplish coloration in much the same fashion as did his predecessors.

The use of skins and feathers predominate in all Indian decoy making and was carried over into the White Man era. My own collection boasts of several examples. In the case of ducks, bodies were made to correspond to the stripped carcass. In applying the skins, wings were removed after the fashion of the Indian. On full bodies, wings only were applied. In White Man decoy making, however, heads were invariably of wood. Many of us recall this system as applied to snipe decoys of the not too distant past. I have examples of them now. These decoys are made of material about one-half inch in thickness with the wings of a snipe tacked on. The result is very effective and of extreme light weight. I confess, however, that after a very short time, they do become odoriferous.

A more permanent extension of Indian methods is illustrated by the "Mallard Head" mounted on a well-made wooden form. This modern "Head Decoy" comes from Saskatchewan, Canada, a type still in frequent use. The method is alleged to have been brought to that region by the early French trappers—coming down from the north. My informant, long resident of the Qui Appel Valley, states that these voyageurs adopted the device from Indians occupying the country at the edge of the Barrens, North West Territory, the Chippeways—most northerly of Indian tribes. But credit must be divided. Similar decoys for the same species were made by predecessors of the Paiutes a thousand, even two thousand years before. That we know.

Aboriginal decoys have all but disappeared but the savage principle remains.

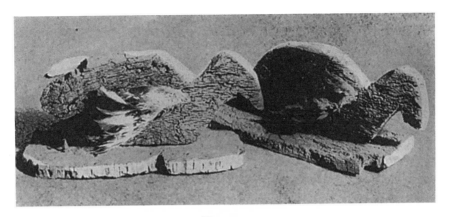

PLATE 29

MODERN OJIBWAY INDIAN DECOYS
Georgian Bay, Canada

PLATE 30

STICK-UP MALLARD HEAD
Saskatchewan, Canada, 1928

PLATE 31
HAWKINS SNIPE *by Ben Hawkins*
Bellport, L. I., about 1800

PLATE 32
BIRD-SKIN BLACK DUCK
Lower Jersey Coast

VII

Decoys of American Duck Shooting

A DECOY, as identified with American duck shooting, may be described as an artificial bird, or more accurately as the likeness of a waterfowl, employed as a lure to entice others to within range of firearms. They are commonly made of wood, painted to simulate species and sex.

Decoys are of two distinct types—one to float on water, the other for use on land. Floating decoys, employed in the shooting of ducks and geese are ballasted by suitable body weight and provided with an anchor for mooring on water. Anchor lines are attached to a fastening on the underside of the breast.

The land decoy is principally used in shore bird shooting, supported in upright position by a removable, leg-like stick seated in the body and thrust into the ground. To distinguish from the floating type, such decoys are designated as "stick-ups." Forerunners of both forms date back to very ancient Indian devices, justifying the claim that such bird lures are indigenous to North America.

The following is a list of Decoyable Birds:

Floating

Canvas-back	Black Duck
Redhead	Mallard
Blue-bill	Pintail

WILD FOWL DECOYS

Floating (Continued)

Brant	Coot (Scoters)
Canada Goose	Ruddy Duck
Whistler	Blue-winged Teal
Mergansers (2)	Green-winged Teal
Widgeon	Buffle-head
Old Squaw	Loon
Eider Duck	Sea Gull

Whistling Swan

Shore Birds and Other Stick-ups

Yellow-leg Snipe	Canada Goose
Black-breasted Plover	Great Blue Heron
Hudsonian Curlew	Passenger Pigeon
Sickle-billed Curlew	Blue-winged Teal
Dowitcher	Sea Gull
Robin Snipe	Crow

English Wood Pigeon

In spite of later importance, the appearance of decoys in the world was an event of too little importance to receive the attentions of historians. But it is of interest to examine conditions and speculate on the manner of its adoption. It is well known that the life of American settlers ran parallel to that of the native Indian, particularly during the days of early colonization. It was therefore inevitable that the newcomer made use of Indian customs current at that period. The artificial bird lure undoubtedly falls in this category. The idea remains unchanged, the only difference being in the method of construction.

It may be observed that through the range of original Indian decoys the use of live birds does not appear. Such a practice would imply the existence of trained or domesticated fowl, and we know that the aboriginal American had no such thing. It is also a fact that Indians continued to employ artificial lures down to the coming of White Men, and later.

Whether the natives had a name for their devices is not

PLATE 33
STICK-UP DECOY, SALTON SEA, LOWER CALIFORNIA, AND
BLUE-WING TEAL *by John Whittaker*
Jamaica Bay, L. I., 1860

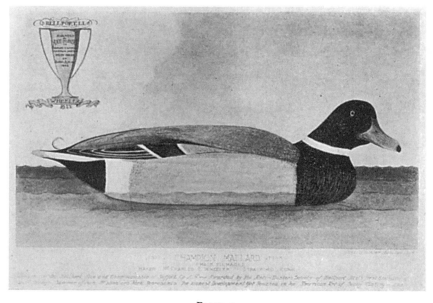

PLATE 34
CHAMPION MALLARD *by Charles E. Wheeler*
Stratford, Conn., 1923

PLATE 35

EARLY TYPES FROM THE AUTHOR'S SKETCH BOOK

known but the White Man's early acquaintance with the custom is a matter of definite historical record.* That the settlers took over the system there can be no doubt, though the manner of adoption is conjectural. Data concerning these early days is scant but what we know to be ancient native methods were employed by White Men at no very distant date. In my own collection are two duck decoys having bodies designed to receive bird-skin covering, also a snipe stool made in 1800 on which bird wings served the purpose of painted plumage. The Mallard head decoy, seen in Plate No. 30, shows the most ancient of Indian methods employed by modern sportsmen in Saskatchewan. Thus in our present-day practice we have parallels of artifices extending back to the beginning of the second period of native American culture; over a thousand years.

First methods of pursuit are also shadowy but from recorded observations it can be assumed that the earliest gunning was conducted from land, ducks and geese being attracted to shore and not killed on open water. But land shooting offered limitations that the increasing demand for waterfowl could not satisfy. The rafts of birds off shore were at once a solution and an inspiration. In response some inventive colonist of unknown name and date, brought forth the innovation that spread rapidly through the colonies. This conjectural person constructed a permanent floating decoy made of wood, which would ride at anchor in semblance of the wild fowl feeding. In this connection, it is important to observe the radical change in construction. While the Indian used materials of an impermanent character, the White Man followed the underlying impulse of his race and employed something relatively permanent—wood. His object was the production of a practical implement for continued and heavy service.

The perfection of this instrument is too well known to require comment. Trifling modifications have appeared, but the

*See "New Voyages to North America." Lahontan, 1687.

great idea remains unchanged and unbeaten after a century of constant use.

These wooden birds of the floating type became known as "Duck Decoys" or "Duck Stool," those of the stick-up variety as "Snipe Decoys" or "Snipe Stool." Both were commonly made of wood and ultimately finished in painted plumage.

As previously outlined, the name Decoy was derived from the process of European fowling. The name Stool likewise comes from old world usages. In its original meaning this latter term signified a movable pole or perch to which a live pigeon was fastened as a lure to entice his kind within gunshot. The bird so used was termed "Stool Pigeon."*

Thus both Decoy and Stool came to designate a device to mislead unwary waterfowl. It is easy to see how these basic but foreign names were applied to the later American invention.†

Along the Atlantic Coast other names appear, principally "Blocks" and even more generally "Tollers." Block is self-explanatory. Toller, while possibly a survival of the process called "Tolling Ducks," in all probability reaches back to the ancient calling or tolling of the death knell. All of these names are still used in different localities, but Decoy, in its original implication of deceit and unseen operator, remains the most generally accepted name for the false bird of American tradition.

From a quite unknown beginning, the making of decoys grew slowly to a stage of minor coastal industry. But it was never more than a slack season trade. Beginning with gunners, it spread to scattered individuals having a peculiar knowledge and knack with tools. All work was done by hand. Practitioners went by the name of "Stool-makers." The years immediately

---

* In recent years and due to the increasing use of live birds to supplement wooden decoys, the latter is now called by the old name of Stool Duck, while the live bird takes back the original designation of Europe, the Decoy Duck. It is of interest to note that after a century of national duck shooting over wooden birds, we head back to the point from which we started.

† The idea of the live stool pigeon was employed extensively in pursuit of the American Wild or Passenger Pigeon, now extinct.

following the Civil War saw the beginning of decoys made by machinery, a separate branch of the industry which continued down to the end of unrestricted shooting. During this period a few well-known factories supplied thousands of decoys to sportsmen and gunners, principally in the south and west.

But the 'longshore stool-maker never ceased production. Handmade decoys were always the favorite of the experienced professional and fastidious sportsman. From this source emanated the epoch-making birds of American duck shooting.

Decoys were the tools of a grim profession. There is no way of estimating the vast number employed in the pursuit of our waterfowl. In the hands of the principal users many were lost every season, broken in necessarily rough handling or going adrift in heavy weather, never to be retrieved. This loss is such a factor that comparatively few decoys made thirty years ago are now extant. Those that do survive are in the class of curios, reminders of an older order of things American which have passed out of existence.

PART IV

PLATE 36
PRIMITIVE BLACK DUCK *by Wilbur R. Corwin*
Bellport, L. I., 1876

PLATE 37
FLOATING SEA GULL *by Capt. Ketchum, Sr.*
Copaigue, L. I., 1860

PLATE 38

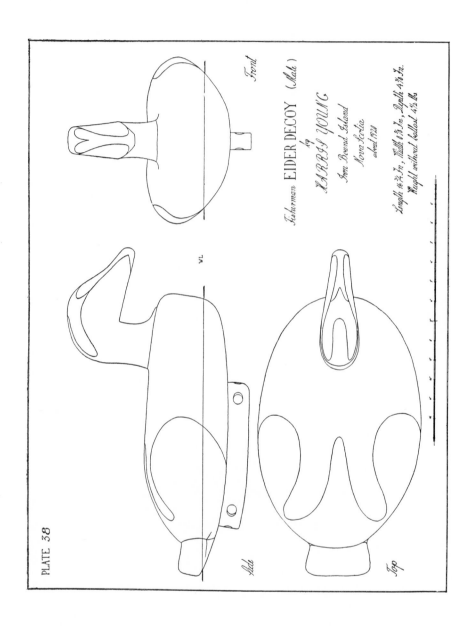

Front

Fisherman EIDER DECOY (Male)
by
HARRY YOUNG
from Brend Island
Nova Scotia
about 1920

Length 16¾ In., Width 8½ In., Depth 4⅛ In.
Weight without ballast 4½ lbs.

WL

Side

Top

VIII

The First Decoy

As one's interest in a given subject becomes known, a general assumption sets in that said interest carries with it a corresponding knowledge. No matter modesty, no matter obscurity, this attitude persists, even to a point of embarrassment.

The question, "Why collect decoy ducks?" is always a poser. One person completely floored me by the query—"What holds them up?" A gentleman to whom I had just been introduced found me completely at a loss when he asked—how many kinds of decoys were made. Well, in spite of owning every kind of decoy from a Dowitcher to a Butcher Cart Goose almost four feet long, I didn't know, had never counted them.

But if such answers are difficult there is one and persistent query that can never be answered:

"Who made the first decoy?"

Real scientists, both by inclination and training, are able to evade things of this sort, but I am less conscientious and more anxious to please. As a result of this purely personal failing, I step to one side and tell the story of another man, an author of the 'forties.

While others have avoided the question, this man definitely commits himself. The account referred to occurs in a volume called *Sporting Scenes and Sundry Sketches,* being the miscellaneous writings of J. Cypress, Jr., published in New York, 1842. The tale from which I shall quote is called "A Week at the Fire Islands." The adventure in part, and supposedly related by a local gunner, runs as follows:

"Why, y' see, th' old man was one o' th' first settlers that come down from M'sschus'tts, and he tuk a small farm on shears down to Fortneck, and he'd everything fixed accorden. The most of his time, hows'm'ver, he spent in the bay, clammen and sich like. He was putty tol'r'bl' smart with a gun, too, and he was the first man that made wooden stools for ducks.

"So he was out bright and arely one morn'n—he'd laid out all night likely—and he'd his stool sot out on th' n'r-east side o' a hassack off Wanza's Flat;—(the place tuk its name from gr't gr'ndf'th'r);—th' wind bein' from the so'-west princip'ly; and he lay in his skiff in the hassack, putty well hid, for't was in th' fall o' the year, and the sedge was smart and high. Well, jest arter day'd fairly broke, and the faawl begun to stir, he reckoned he heer'd a kind o' splashen in the water, like geese pick'n and wash'n themselves. So he peeked through the grass, softly, to see where the flock was; but, 'stead o' geese, he see a queer looken old feller waden 'long on the edge o' th' flat, jest by th' channel, benden low down, with a bow and arr in his hands, all fixed, ready to shoot, and his eye upon gr't gr'ndf'th'r's stool. 'That feller thinks my stool's faawl,' says the old man to himself, softly, 'cause he 'xpected the fell'r was an Ingen, and there wa'n't no tellen whether he was friendly or not, in them times. So he sot still and watched. The bow and arr kept goen on, and to rights it stopped. Then the feller what had it, ris up, and pulled string, and let slip. Slap went the arr, strut into one o' gr't gr'ndf'th'r's broadbills, and stuck fast, shaken. The old man sniggled as he see th' other feller pull, and then jump and splash thro' th' water to pick up his game, but he said nothen. Well, the merm'n,—as it turned out to be,—got to th' stool, and he seemed most won'rf'll s'prized th' birds didn't get up and fly, and then he tuk up the br'db'll and pulled out his arr, and turned the stool ov'r and ov'r, and smelt it, and grinned, and seemed quite uneasy to make out what 'twas. Then he tuk up nother one, and he turned 'em putty much all ov'r, and tore their anchors loose.

"Gr't gr'ndf'thr wa'n't a bit skeered, and he didn't like this much, but he didn't want to git into a passion with an Ingen, for they're full o' fight, and he loved peace; and besides he didn't want to take no dis'dvantage of 'im, and he'd two guns loaded in th' skiff, and th' other feller hadn't only a bow and arr, and the old man hoped he'd clear out soon. It wa'n't to be, hows'mver, that the old man shouldn't get int' a scrape; for what's the feller with the bow and arr do, arter consideren and smellen a smart and long spell, but pick up the whole stool,— every one on 'em,—and sling 'em ov'r's shoulder, and begin to make tracks! Gr't gr'ndf'th's couldn't stand that ere. So he sung out to him, putty loud and sharp, to lay down them stools, and he shoved the skiff out the hassack, and then he see plain enough it was a merm'n. Then the old man was a little started, I expect. Hows'mver, he shoved right up to him, and got his old muskets ready. Well, the merm'n turned round, and sich another looken mortal man gr't gr'ndf'th'r said he never did see. He'd big bushy hair all ov'r 'im, and big whiskers, and his eyes was green and small's a mushrat's, and where the flesh was, he was ruther scaly-like.

"He hadn't stich clothes ont' 'm, but the water was up to's waist, and kivered 'im up so that gr't gr'ndf'th'r couldn't see the biggist part on 'im. Soon's the old man got down jawen, the merm'n he begun to talk out the darndest talk you ever heerd. I disremember 'xactly, but I b'lieve 'twas somethin' like 'norgus porgus carry-Yorkus,' and all sich stuff. Ephr'm Salem, the schoolmaster, used to reckon 'twas Lating, and meant somethin' 'bout takin' load o' porgees down to York; other some said 'twas Dutch; but I can't say. Well, the old man let him talk his talk out, and then he took his turn. Says the old man says he, 'it ant respect'ble, 'tant honest, mister merm'n, to hook other people's property. Them's my stools,' says he. 'Ye lie,' says the merm'n,—speakin' so gr't gr'ndf'th'r could hear 'im plain enough when he cum to the pint;—'ye lie,' says he, 'I jest now shot 'em.'

" 'Shot 'em, you b . . . ,' says the old man, gittin' mad; 'shot 'em? Them's wooden stools what I made myself an anchored 'em here last night.'

" 'That's 'nother,' says the merm'n; 'ye blackguard, they're only dead ducks spetrerfried, and turned into white oak.' "

This is an admirable story and however legendary in character, of real historical value. Written nearly a hundred years ago, it gives credit to one particular man for making the first decoy. However contestable that claim, the fact of publication in 1842 indicates that the device, at that time was in sufficiently general use to warrant the assumption of many readers who would understand and approve the tale. It may also be implied that decoys had been in existence so many years that an account concerning origin, would be reasonably correct with respect to date. This date, the great-grandfather's time, is authenticated by less inspired but more serious record. According to legend, therefore, the mythical first decoy of American duck shooting came into existence before the Revolution.

PLATE 39

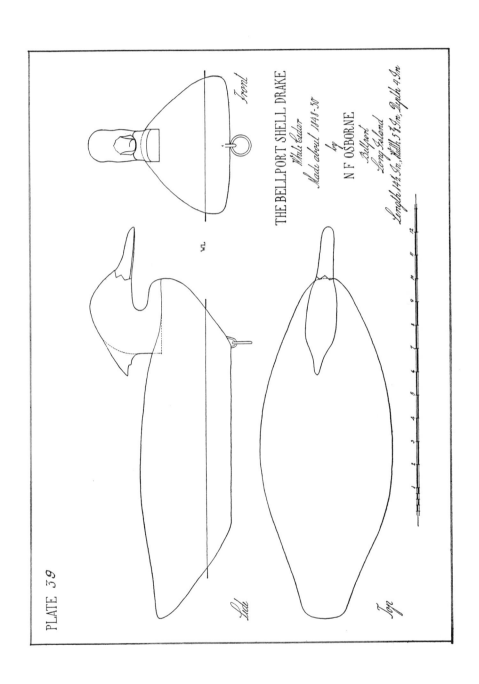

Front

WL

THE BELLPORT SHELL DRAKE
White Cedar
Made about 1848-50
by
N F OSBORNE
Bellport
Long Island
Length 14½ In, Width 5⅝ In, Depth 4 In.

Side

Top

PLATE 40
CLEVELAND CANVAS-BACK
North East, Md., about 1880

PLATE 41
GREY COOT *by Capt. Gilbert Davis*
Annisquam, Mass., about 1870

IX

Printed Records

It is not to be supposed that the beginning of decoys in America is a matter of definite record. Far from it. Up to 1870, it is necessary to rely on scattered references dealing only with the existence of the device. From this date on, such information can be supplemented by the testimony of gunners and decoy makers now living. Actual details of origin and process of development lie far beyond reach of long memories. Early history, therefore, can be based only on meagre printed reports.

For the most part these data are contained in old books on American wild fowl shooting, supplemented by notice in contemporary works on natural history. It is my purpose here to assemble this information in chronological order and by so doing, form a consistent record of available data. Such a procedure will establish the introduction of decoys into American wild fowling and indicate, as definitely as possible, localities where first used.

As the earliest mention of American decoys occurs in a work on Natural History—the first edition of *Wilson's American Ornithology,* published in 1808–1814—to this celebrated naturalist goes the credit of original observation as to the existence of artificial birds. The actual passage, under heading of "The Mallard" runs as follows:

1808, 1814

"In some ponds frequented by these birds, five or six wooden figures, cut and painted so as to represent ducks, and sunk, by pieces of lead nailed on their bottoms, so as to float at the usual depth on the surface, are anchored in a favorable position for being raked from concealment of brush, etc., on the shore. The appearance of these usually attracts passing flocks, which alight and are shot down. Sometimes eight or ten of these painted wooden ducks are fixed on a wooden frame in various swimming postures, and secured to the bow of the gunner's skiff, projecting before it in such a manner that the weight of the frame sinks the figures to their proper depth . . ."

It is possible that earlier printed or written mention exists, but if so, I am not acquainted with it. In addition to the fact of existence, this report shows that "wooden figures," cut and painted to resemble ducks, were employed in pursuit of Mallards, birds frequenting shoal water.

Though "tolling" and "flight shooting" were widely practiced at this time, the tide of decoys was rising. This is evidenced by the following passage which occurs in *The American Shooter's Manual,* published in 1827.*

1827

"Hogsheads are sometimes sunk into the mud on the flats over which the birds fly, in which the shooter and his dog are concealed. Artificial ducks, and stool ducks are also employed to decoy these poor birds, and no trick, or stratagem that human ingenuity can devise for their destruction, is left untried."

At this time, the use of decoys in the Chesapeake Bay region was little known. This is evidenced by a passage in *The Cabinet of Natural History,* published in Philadelphia in 1830. This reference appearing in a chapter entitled "Chesapeake Duck Shooting" is as follows:

1830

"Stool ducks are little known, and from the very partial success in their employment last fall, by the writer and his company, their usefulness seems very problematical."

* "The American Shooter's Manual," by a gentleman of Philadelphia County. Published at Philadelphia in 1827.

PRINTED RECORDS

The next printed mention of decoys is chronicled by a brief passage in *A Manual of the Ornithology of the United States and of Canada,* which appeared in 1832. Again under the heading "Common Duck, or Mallard" is the following:

1832

"It would far exceed our limits to detail the various arts employed in order to obtain this widely and highly esteemed game. Decoys of wood, carefully painted to imitate these and other species, are sometimes very successful lures in the morning twilight. The imitation of floating objects, as a boat painted white among the moving ice, has also sometimes been attended with complete success."

From the early 'fifties, references to the use of decoys occur principally in connection with Canvas-back shooting as practiced on Chesapeake Bay. This bird and locality are inseparable and have long been a favorite subject of sportsmen and sporting writers. In evidence of this point of view, let me quote Mr. John Krider, gunmaker, sportsman and author. In his *Sporting Anecdotes,* published in Philadelphia in 1853, under the heading "Wild Fowl" he observes:

1853

"Proudly pre-eminent among the water-fowl of the United States, for the elegance of its plumage, the exquisite flavor of its flesh, and the sport which it affords the shooter, stands the far famed Canvas-back. Gentle reader, if you have ever lain submerged in a battery on Devil's Island, or in ambuscade in the narrows of Spesutia, and watched them pitching, in their superb way, among your decoys, or bent to your oars on a blustering day, and snatched them from the rough waters of the Chesapeake; or studied the markings of their winter dress, as they lay upon the thwart-board of the scow in pairs of fifty at a time, and finally, if you have sailed, poled or swept back to Havre de Grace by the light of the moon—dropped anchor and gone on shore to dine upon them cooked *Au Naturel*—then, perhaps, you have realized to its fullest extent, the spell contained in those potent words—CANVAS-BACK."

Notwithstanding statements of later observers, perusal of these "Anecdotes" shows conclusively that decoys were in general and popular use on the Chesapeake at this time. From Mr. Krider's very excellent description of battery shooting I quote from his description of the "New Scow" which he (the host) had built and equipped after the most approved manner, especially to kill ducks in the Susquehanna and the Upper Bay:

"Midships rested the battery or 'sunk box,' of which we shall soon have occasion to speak, and piled up in great heaps abaft on either side, but so as not to interfere with the motions of the rudder, were the decoys or wooden ducks, each having its cord with the weight attached, wound round its body, the last turn being taken round the neck, regular duck-shooter fashion. They had evidently seen service from their bleached and weathered looks. Some of them bore the appearance of having been recently prettily peppered in the way of business."

The information and observations of this author are of great interest. Near the end of the chapter he remarks: "Taking up some two hundred decoys on a cold, blustering evening, is rather tedious and benumbing work to the novice," showing first-hand knowledge of the now-familiar hardships of battery shooting.

The rapid development of decoys on the Chesapeake during the 'fifties has led to the supposition that this home of decoys was the place of birth. Evidence at hand, however, points elsewhere. In a chapter devoted to Canvas-back shooting on these famous waters, Dr. Lewis records incidents of battery shooting and the use of decoys during 1846 and 1847. On the subject of origin, however, he makes this pertinent observation:*

1855

"This system (battery shooting) was introduced on the Chesapeake Bay by some of the experienced wild-fowl shooters from the vicinity of New York, and who now reap a rich harvest from their hardihood and ingenuity. It is no unusual thing for one of

* Elisha J. Lewis, "Lewis's American Sportsman." Published at Philadelphia, 1885.

these men to kill as many as fifty couples of Canvas-backs in the course of a day; and if the weather prove favorable for this kind of shooting, they have been known to fill a small vessel with ducks in two or three days, which they immediately dispatch for the markets of New York, Baltimore or Philadelphia."

The foregoing quotation implies that battery shooting and decoys did not originate on the Chesapeake but were introduced there by fowlers from the vicinity of New York. In further evidence of this supposition I quote a passage from Frank Forester's *Complete Manual for Young Sportsmen.** Although Dr. Lewis specifically tells of battery shooting and decoys in use during the seasons of 1846–47, Forester describes contemporary methods of duck shooting as follows:

1856

"The method of shooting wild-fowl on the Chesapeake Bay is to wait for them as they fly up and down . . . behind screens erected for the purpose on the points and islands which they must necessarily pass and shoot them on the wing. Another method much employed in this paradise of duck shooters, is to toll the ducks, as it is called, while they are feeding along the shore, quite out of range, into a shooting distance of the ambushed fowler, by means of a dog trained to gamble along the bank."

He also mentions that paddling up to birds in canoes on the feeding ground, sailing onto them or firing with swivels, as being "unworthy of gentlemen."

He then describes in detail and deplores the battery shooting of Long Island, the familiar sink box with its "fleet of decoys of all kinds and sizes, exactly representing all varieties of fowl which he may expect, riding at anchor around him."

In respect to Jersey waters, although equally clear on the subject of batteries, he is much less definite on the subject of decoys. "On Jersey waters," relates Forester, "Squam Beach and Barnegat, and other places of equal resort of wild fowl,

*Frank Forester, "Complete Manual for Young Sportsmen." First published in 1856.

prohibition of this destructive machine is on the whole en-forced by the natives, a half-piratical race, half-fowlers, half-fishermen, and more than half-wreckers."

Thus again the use of batteries and decoys is noted as being in general use on Long Island, while no mention of decoys appears in connection with the gunning on the Chesapeake or the Jersey waters designated as "off Squam Beach and Barnegat."

From these scanty records it would appear that the wooden decoy was first recorded in the year 1814, and used in connection with the shooting of Mallards. In 1830 decoys were little known on the Chesapeake, but according to a *Manual of the Ornithology of the United States,* "decoys of wood" were carefully painted to imitate Mallard and other species.

Then among the miscellaneous writings of J. Cypress, Jr., appears the man on the south shore of Long Island who in jocular fashion claims the distinction of making the first decoy for a great-grandfather who came from Massachusetts. We may also assume that the battery and its fleet of decoys was carried to the Chesapeake by gunners from the "vicinity of New York." Authentic data on the introduction of decoys in America are limited to these meagre facts, pointing to middle Atlantic coastal origin at the beginning of the nineteenth century. The inventor and exact locality lay in utter oblivion.

PLATE 42

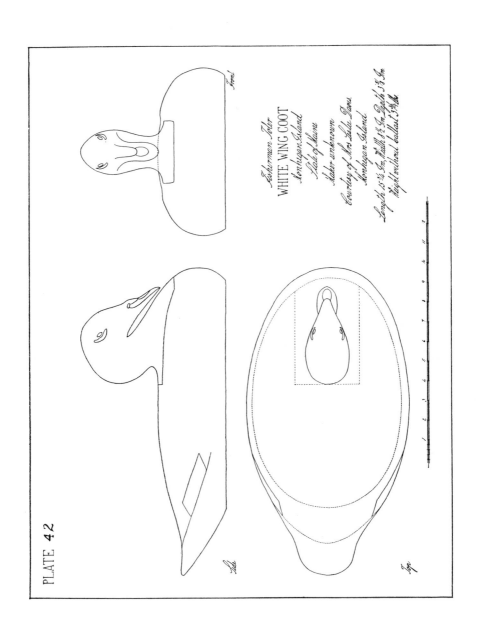

Fisherman Tyler
WHITE WING COOT
Newbigan Island
Lake of Maine
Maker unknown
Courtesy of Mrs Lulu Davis,
Monhegan Island
Length 15¼ In., Width 8½ In., Depth 5½ In.
Weight without ballast 5¼ lbs.

Front

Side

Top

PLATE 43
CORK BLACK DUCK *by Thomas Gelston*
Quogue, L. I., 1897

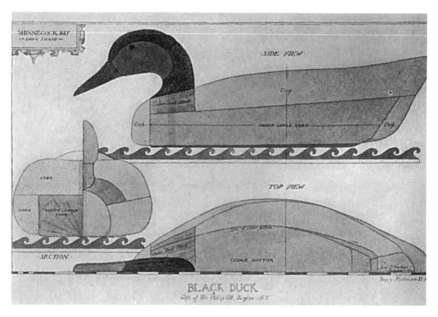

PLATE 44
VENEERED CORK BLACK DUCK
Shinnecock Bay, L. I.

X

Early Decoys

IN DISCUSSING "early decoy making," it is fitting to give first place to the "stick-up"—undoubtedly the prototype of the American decoy. There can be no question that this more primitive device preceded the invention of floating lures and was employed not only for shore birds but for ducks and geese as well. It is also probable that birds were first attracted to land and not killed on open water. Subsequent to the appearance of floating decoys, the stick-up has become associated with shore bird shooting but as this type of fowling is quite distinct from the larger activity of "duck shooting" the so-called snipe decoys will be treated in another chapter.

The stick-up duck decoy has all but disappeared from modern gunning, but the principle continues in the profile geese decoys so generally used on the cut-over wheat fields of the Western States and the sand bars of the Mississippi River. Here in a continuance of the original "dry-land" gunning of water birds the ancient stick-up decoy continues to function.

Being quite outmoded by the more effective floating decoy, very few stick-up ducks are now extant. In Plate No. 33, I show two examples from widely separated localities; one from the shore of Jamaica Bay, the other from the Salton Sea, in Southern California.

Decoys constructed on this principle had serious limitations. While made of permanent material, their use was confined to land or at best shoal water. On water, however, they would not remain upright unless a support were thrust deep in the bottom, and, even so, were in danger of being carried away by visiting tides or rough seas. This objection could only be removed by the introduction of a floating lure, held in place by an anchor, and thus permitting the use of decoys in the quarry's natural habitat.

The process of change from stick-up to floating decoy is wholly without evidence, but one of many surmises has real support; that the bodies of two unstable decoys were attached to either end of a short board or float. This arrangement, similar in principle to the catamaran, gave relative stability and insured an upright position. According to 'longshore gossip this device had its origin along the coast of New England.

It is possible that in making the first of these double decoys, former stick-ups were employed, but the original idea may also have been of an even more primitive character. To illustrate this assumption I admit a description of the so-called log goose shown in Plate No. 35.

This queer looking catamaran is pure conjecture, the sketch being made from vague but persistent coastal rumors of its existence. But it is really an excellent idea. Two logs, cut to the desired length, are fastened together by two short poles or stretchers tenoned into auger holes near the ends. Heads are cut from suitably formed saplings on which a short section of branch is retained to act the part of the bill. Heads are secured to the bodies by shaping the neck or standing part and driving into auger holes on the forward ends. The only tools required are an axe and an auger, but the resultant decoy is quite satisfactory. The very simplicity of construction is convincing.

"The Catamaran Goose" may or may not be a legitimate ancestor of deep-water decoys, but the principle has existing and well-known applications. Chief among these are the profile or shadow decoys so generally used in gunning Coot off the New England coast; see Plate No. 76.

In constructing these decoys, profiles of the complete duck are cut from one-inch boards and supported by stretcher pieces from two to three feet long and nailed to the bottoms. The stretchers between the two profiles are frequently made in graduated lengths to permit of nesting together and so facilitate stowing in the gunning dory.

Old-time Brant gunners had another application of the idea called "Outriggers." In the days of Spring Shooting, many rigs included "Tip-ups." The word itself is descriptive, meaning a cone-like decoy painted white in imitation of bird tipping up or diving for food. In some instances tip-ups were anchored individually but in most cases were located at one end of a board about two feet long, occupied at the other end by a complete decoy.

Among the earliest references to the use of wooden decoys in America will be found record of another method of stabilizing decoys, the use of "frames." In the "Goose Stand" shooting of eastern Massachusetts the frame system is still employed. This type of gunning calls for huge decoys, described by my friend John Phillips as being "as big as a barrel." These super lures are geese decoys having bodies planked up on frames as in boat construction, but unlike a boat the bottom is left open. For support, these skeleton forms are attached to huge triangular frames of poles, one decoy at each apex of the triangle. The groups thus formed are moored by an anchor line attached to the frame.

Different localities have variations of this principle to accomplish stability. The idea is very old and mentioned in the first printed reference to the use of decoys in America. One of the most widely used is in the form of a cross employed on the deep waters of Long Island Sound. These crosses carry four and sometimes eight decoys on its arms.

But the use of frames to maintain decoys in position was not confined to the waters of New England. Only a few years ago I found one myself in the loft of a barn on the shore of the Elk

River, Maryland. It is impressed on my memory because spiked fast to one of its sides was the finest Pintail decoy I had ever seen. The head was in bad repair and the decoy had been painted a dirty black all over, but nothing could disguise the beauty of line or portraiture. I was informed that the frame had been used the preceding season on the waters of the Elk River with considerable success.

In discussing early methods of making individual floating decoys we first encounter evidence of men now living. For the following account of decoy making in the middle 'forties, I am indebted to Dr. William Bruette, for many years editor of the famous but now discontinued *Forest and Stream*.

It appears that Dr. Bruette's grandfather, resident of Flushing, Long Island, owned extensive lands in what is now the State of Wisconsin. The property was located in a paradise of game including myriads of wild fowl. During the late 'forties, the elder Bruette spent a portion of each year on the property and instituted the Long Island custom of shooting ducks over decoys. The story of how these were made comes down as one of the family gunning legends. The method of making, no doubt, was inspired by customs established in the East.

These Wisconsin decoys were made from over-sized butts cut from white cedar poles used for the growing of hops, one of the principal crops of the locality. The round timber was cut in lengths and split in halves, thus furnishing material for two decoy bodies. On the convex side, near the end, an auger hole was bored to receive the head, consisting of a peg or "plug" driven securely into the hole. The head plugs were set at slightly different angles giving semblance of varied poses. The sketch in Plate No. 35 shows the idea more clearly than words.

What might be described as the last step in early methods comes in the form of first-hand testimony. My informant, Captain Al Ketchum of Copiague, Long Island, tells of decoy

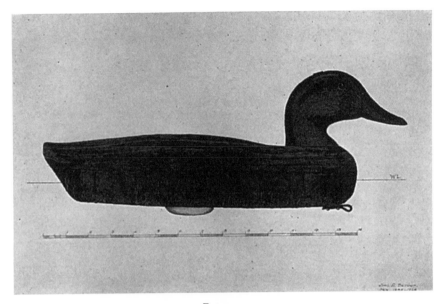

PLATE 45
MODERN CORK BLACK DUCK *by Ralph M. Cranford*
Babylon, L. I.

PLATE 46
From a Drawing by Joseph W. Long, in "American Wild Fowl Shooting," 1874

SLEEPING BROADBILL *by Laing*　　　BLACK DUCK *by Benjamin Holmes*
PLATE 47
Stratford, Conn., about 1870

PLATE 48
HOLLOW MALE WHISTLER
Stratford, Conn., about 1880

making as practiced by the baymen and gunners of his youth. The story deals with the extensive market shooting of Brant during his father's and grandfather's time in the 'sixties.

The shooting referred to by Captain Ketchum was conducted in the spring, from so-called "Brant boxes" on the flats, east of Amityville, L. I. The original boxes were not floating batteries but described as much deeper and stationary, accommodating two gunners. When occupied they required constant bailing, and were often completely flooded by high tides. As a boy, when first allowed to accompany the older men, it was Captain Ketchum's duty to "load guns" and "keep the box bailed out."

Captain Al's recollections of decoy making by father and grandfather were very clear and instructive. Bodies were made from seasoned white cedar fence rails, roughly hewn to shape with an axe and fitted with heads cut from pine knots.* Heads were not nailed to bodies but fitted and driven into auger holes. The entire process was conducted out-of-doors at a chopping block. There was no pointing. New decoys were brought to uniform color by charring in a fire, and allowed to weather. In course of time underbodies were painted white to "brighten up the rig." But the oldest decoys were very crude and left piled on the shore when not in use, "the year around."

That we have so few observers of the Captain Ketchum type is regrettable. For his kind of history has a quality of its own. As the result of our talk that day he presented me with an old Labrador Gull of the floating type formerly used in Brant shooting. The gull was older than his memory, beautifully made but shabby and grey with age. This gull, it appears, was always used in company with the Brant decoys, anchored off one side of the main rig to give further assurance that all was well at the ambush. Like the memory of that juvenile gunner it is highly prized. It is always reminiscent of a shivering boy, crouching at the feet of father and grandfather, in the

* For description of decoy heads made from pine knots, see next Chapter.

bottom of a hazy "box"; alternately bailing and loading guns in a desperate effort to stop the tide of birds. Every time I see that gull I hear again the end of his story. "Why, some nights, Mr. Barber, I couldn't hear at all, from the shooting over my head all day."

Author's Note

The Brant shooting referred to in Captain Ketchum's account was conducted in the spring of the year. At that season the Brant is subject to attraction by decoys, and was a bird of considerable economic importance. Since the prohibition of spring shooting, 1913, the killing of Brant has ceased to be a factor of importance; they do not decoy well in the fall.

PART V

PLATE A
GUNNERS' PLUMAGE PATTERNS

WHISTLER

BLUE-BILL

MALLARD

JOEL BARBER '34

XI

Decoy Making

SOLID DECOYS

THE ACTUAL PROCESS of making decoys is of misleading simplicity. In order to succeed it is necessary to have a queer sort of knowledge, augmented by so-called talent; things quite impossible to convey by description. There are two principal methods of construction, solid decoys having bodies cut from a single block and hollow decoys with the body built up of two or more sections and hollowed out. Beyond these two basic types come minor variations which will be treated under another chapter.

Of all types, the solid decoy is the most important. It has maintained its popularity with duck shooters throughout the whole period of American wild fowling. It is still used on all waters where birds are gunned, and for gunning on deep water is unsurpassed. From Nova Scotia, southward along the entire Atlantic Coast, up the Mississippi River and northward into Canada, decoys of the solid type are still considered the best. They ride on graplin anchors over New England shoals, in fifteen fathoms of water. They lie at anchor on the Susquehanna Flats, Currituck Sound or Great South Bay. At home in all waters, they uphold the traditions of American duck shooting. Over this type of decoy more birds have been killed and more powder burned than all other kinds of decoys put together.

In the category of solid decoys are to be found the likenesses of every species of wild fowl, subject to attraction by means of floating lures. In my own collection there are examples varying in size from the small Ruddy Duck, weighing only a few ounces, up to the huge Maryland Swan which weighs fifteen pounds. In the category of these decoys are found ducks, geese, gulls, swans and other birds in manifold variety.

In a previous chapter I have already given a description of early methods of making decoys and it is proper to describe here the methods which were perfected about the time of the Civil War, and although certain improvements have been made since that time, the process of making solid wooden decoys established then has persisted to our own days.

The first operations are major ones and rapidly effected. Yet casual as the process may appear, there are comparatively few men who possess the characteristics which fit them to become real decoy makers. No mere diagrams nor descriptions can convey to others the subtle quality possessed by such workmen. One must see their actual handiwork to appreciate it. Yet, in order to preserve for posterity a record of the peculiar trade of these decoy makers, one can only resort to the means provided by the pencil and pen.

Decoy making has four distinct divisions: body making, head making, assembling and painting. Supplementary to these there are two minor operations, which taken together, are classified as rigging. Rigging includes the attaching of necessary body weight or ballast, also the anchor line and fastening.

A decoy consists of two parts, body and head. The material most in favor at the present day is native white pine. In earlier times white cedar was employed but is no longer available. This pine is nowadays purchased in standard mill sizes. Body material for ducks is generally $4'' \times 6''$ in section; head material is $1\frac{3}{8}''$ or $1\frac{3}{4}''$ planking, preferably of the latter thickness.

The maker, in starting to work, first cuts the $4'' \times 6''$ body material into exact lengths as required by his own standard decoys. When a number of these blocks are piled ready for use, he proceeds to hew the blocks into more or less rough semblance of the bird's body. For this purpose he uses a very sharp carpenter's hatchet and works on a chopping block of convenient height. In this operation the four lateral corners of the block are rapidly hewn away, the tail is worked down to form, and the breast also roughly shaped. Some makers carry the work at the chopping block further than others, but they all invariably carry each successive body to the same state of completion as they proceed. When the allotted number of blocks are so roughed out, the maker takes his next step. In this operation the hewn bodies, held by means of a vise, are rapidly brought to final and uniform shape by the dextrous use of a long, narrow-bladed draw-knife. In accomplishing this, the maker uses no pattern or template, but depends entirely upon his skill and his trained eye to achieve his standard shape. All the bodies are fashioned with a slightly over-size flat area at the forward end, this area being of the correct height and pitch to receive the head.

The making of decoy heads is frequently done at odd times by the decoy maker, but its description may properly follow that of making the bodies. The heads require more care for their fashioning than do the bodies. Nowadays they are sawed to shape on a band saw and the decoy maker's work actually begins with these block-like heads. They are invariably sawed according to a pattern or template furnished by the maker. Head patterns vary, yet the pattern used by any particular maker for a certain species of bird is quite personal and he uses the same template for all decoys of that species. The first step in head making usually consists of boring the sawed blocks to facilitate the fastening of the head to the body by dowel or spike. The blocks are then placed in a vise and by the use of a small-bladed draw-knife, the block is roughly shaped. This preliminary cutting is carried to a uniform state of completion as in the case of bodies. The final cutting or finishing to exact shape is done with a jack-knife, or, in some cases, by a knife made from a razor-blade. The heads, in this whittled condition, are considered completed, though showing knife marks. It is of interest to note, relative to the production of these heads, that under pressure, certain workmen can complete as many as thirty—or even forty—heads in one day. The number produced is limited only by the length of time the man can hold a knife and operate it.

The two parts, body and head, are next assembled. The most approved fastening consists of a long iron spike, supplemented by minor nailing of the head base. I am led to say this because of the fact that such metal fastenings are not affected adversely by water as are wooden dowels. In order that the head may be fastened securely, the flat section on the forward end of the body is dressed off with a small plane, thus providing a perfect bearing. The head is then spiked in place by means of a single five-inch galvanized iron finishing nail which passes down through the center of the head, and it is further secured by means of a similar nail about 2½″ long, which passes through the back of the head. These nails or spikes are driven securely into the body and the nail-heads are counter-sunk. One or two small copper nails are then applied to secure the forward part of the head plate.

To complete the assembling, the decoy is again placed in a vise and the body is given its final and fair surfacing by means of a spoke-shave. After this, both body and head are sandpapered to remove tool marks. The decoy is now ready for painting.

At a surprisingly early date, it became the fashion to equip decoys with artificial eyes. The custom was confined chiefly to the higher grade factory product or to handmade decoys of smaller and rather special rigs. The professional gunners of the coast never adopted the idea, holding steadily to painted eyes or none at all. The most desirable type were the glass eyes of taxidermy. Chief among the substitutes were "tack eyes," oval headed brass nails and "shoe button eyes." Eyes were

PLATE 49

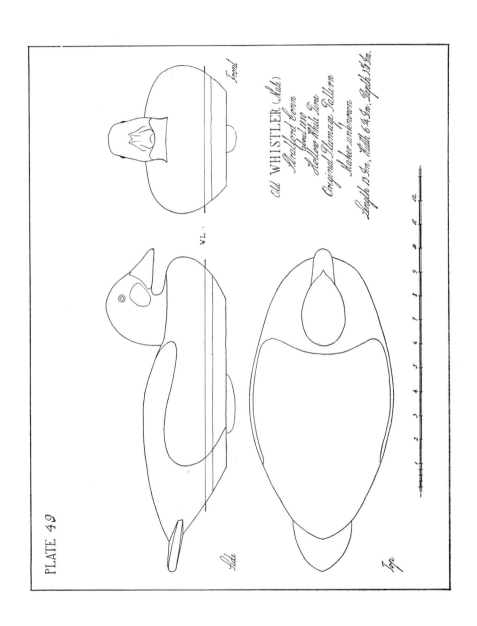

Old WHISTLER (Male)

Stratford Conn.
about 1900
Hollow White Pine
Original Plumage Pattern
by
Maker unknown

Length 13 In., Width 6 ¼ In., Depth 5 ½ In.

Front

WL.

Side

Top

PLATE 50

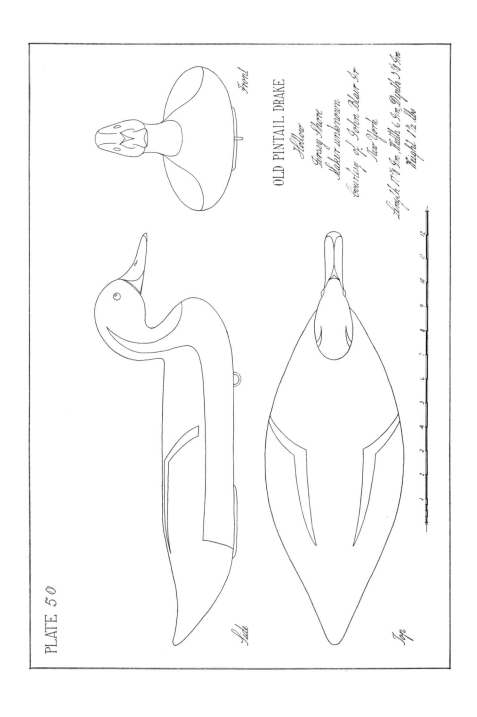

Front

Side

Top

OLD PINTAIL DRAKE
Yellow
Jersey Shore
Maker unknown
Courtesy of John Blair Jr
New York
Length 17 ¾ In, Width 6 In, Depth 3 ½ In
Weight 1 ½ lbs

also indicated by incised carving. Glass eyes and shoe buttons were countersunk and set in white lead after the smoothing process. Most makers applied these accessories before painting.

The painting is done preferably in one continuous operation. Sometimes the pattern is indicated in pencil, or the decoy maker may lay out his work as he proceeds. His palette, so to speak, is an established one; his colors are chosen definitely in accordance with his personal predilections, and his brushes are chosen with respect to size for each color and each painting operation. Holding the decoy by the head and resting it amidship the decoy maker paints the tail and after part of the body. As he turns the decoy to reach all sides, it is moved forward towards the edge of the bench. As he proceeds towards the head, applying the standard colors, the decoy is supported and turned on its tail. When the painting and shading reaches the bill, he swings the decoy to a suitable and convenient rack, using the bill as the one dry spot by which it may be handled. The decoy now is at rest on the open rack, and this remaining portion is painted.

The method of painting here described is varied by some decoy makers who do their painting in two distinct operations: painting the complete body first and then painting the head after the body is thoroughly dry. In the repainting of decoys, however, the method first described is generally followed. Some decoy makers maintain that new decoys should first receive a priming coat of lead and oil, not only to protect the wood but to provide a proper foundation for the plumage pattern. Personally, however, I prefer the direct application of finish color to the raw wood, inasmuch as the decoy will never show any color foreign to the pattern when it is marred in handling. If eyes are required they are painted on, either by means of a small brush, or by the employment of a tube wet with the proper color and applied as a stamp.

Decoy painting has two rather special angles: the actual

pattern or type of plumage to be painted, and painting in such a way as to eliminate the artificial sheen produced by the use of paint, particularly when wet. Many degrees of naturalistic painting have developed in recent years but its use is very restricted. In some quarters the value of elaboration is sincerely questioned. It is said to introduce qualities unnecessary to the requirements of a decoy. In the hands of a few men, however, this feather painting is an art; a movement of great interest and a natural development of decoy making. With respect to utilitarian decoys, the old and simpler patterns of painting still persist. And some of these designs are very fine; with all their apparent crudeness, they reproduce the protective coloration of nature. They also have the practical advantage of easy repainting.

Apparently the various patterns were arrived at through a process of evolution, a camouflage of the highest type and thus of historical interest. The worth of these patterns must be acknowledged when the same designs were arrived at by men in widely separated localities.

The application of colors is a much disputed division of decoy making. In painting decoys for use in salt or brackish water, standard lead and oil paint is used. Once overboard the artificial sheen resulting from the oil, soon disappears. Continuous exposure improves them.

In painting decoys for black duck, and other wary species, it is desirable to exercise more care. One formula, and highly recommended, is the use of color ground in Japan with turpentine instead of oil as a medium. To this mixture is added spar varnish in such quantity as to "fix" the color without causing sheen or gloss. It is well to remember that in all decoy painting, the result should be dull and quiet—almost to the point of invisibility as in the coloring of nature.*

There still remains the application of ballast, the anchor

---

* Some decoy makers paint in the afternoon and leave their work outdoors through the night, claiming that a fall of dew on the fresh paint helps to deaden its sheen.

and line with suitable fastening on the breast. These accessories are usually supplied and attached by the gunner to suit his special ideas and requirements. It is a matter quite separate from the usual work of the maker and will be treated in a special chapter.

XII

Cork and Balsa Wood Decoys

THE SOLID DECOY cut from blocks of white pine or cedar has been the standard for many years. For the heavy duty of battery shooting and other forms of deep-water gunning its merit is unquestioned. But for duck shooting on sheltered waters, heavy decoys may justifiably be replaced by decoys still solid but of lighter material, and thus more convenient to handle.

The most important of these light weight solid decoys is the cork decoy. In these the bodies are made principally of natural cork. The originator of this type is unknown, but to the best of my belief, cork decoys made their first appearance in the early part of the present century on Great South Bay. The early cork types were, without exception, Black Duck with bodies built up of two layers of life-preserver cork salvaged on the beaches. They were flat bottomed and crudely shaped. The two layers of cork were pinned together with white cedar pegs or meat skewers. The heads were made of white pine, secured to the bodies by a wood dowel ⅜″ in diameter. The bodies, after being finished off with a rasp, were lightly sand-papered, then brushed with kerosene and burned. Later on the use of kerosene was abandoned and the bodies charred by means of a gasolene paint torch. After a very short time in use the natural cork, treated in this fashion, takes on the beautiful and dusky texture of the Black Duck plumage. The heads were painted according to the prevailing practice.

PLATE 51
SLEEPING BLACK DUCK
From City Island, N. Y., of Connecticut origin

PLATE 52
OLD SNIPE *by Capt. John Whittaker*
Jamaica Bay, L. I., about 1850

PLATE 53
GROUP OF SHORE-BIRDS. See Text.

PLATE 54
GROUP OF STICK-UP DECOYS. See Text.

CORK AND BALSA WOOD DECOYS

The earliest of these decoys were equipped with a wooden keel running the entire length of the body; the keel being about seven-eighths inch thick by one and one-half to two inches deep. The lead body weight was attached to the keel and the keel furnished with a hole at the forward end to receive the anchor line.

During recent years the use of cork by Long Island makers has been extended and is used in the making of other species, principally for Broad-bill and Geese. The lightness of the material and its ability to withstand the damaging effects of water are most desirable factors. The natural cork, however, is an expensive thing from which to make decoys. It varies in thickness from an inch to two inches with imperfections and lack of uniformity. In cutting out the forms, the unavoidable waste is an important factor.

The accompanying drawings and diagrams show typical decoys of this material. Its use calls for very simple handling of body forms but that in itself is an excellent feature. Due to an average thickness of one and one-half inches, decoy bodies of this type are seldom more than three inches deep and frequently less. In most cases they are of the flat-bottom type and carry a keel.

Once familiar with the material the process of working cork proceeds rapidly. The forms for the body are sawn roughly to shape and surfaced for joining with a coarse rasp. The two halves are then cemented and pegged together and the cement permitted to set. After this the final shape is worked out with a coarse rasp and finished with sandpaper. The charring of the body is usually the next step to avoid scorching those parts which are to be painted. If necessary to re-burn the surface, the head is wrapped in a wet cloth for protection.

The head is fastened to the body with a dowel reinforced by pegs or cut nails in the forward part of base. Cement is also employed to insure a tight and proper joint. The keel is secured by wooden pegs and if properly applied will never come away.

[75]

To accomplish this it is necessary to set pegs at a slight pitch from a common center. An undersized hole should be bored for each peg to permit of proper driving. Fastenings of this kind will hold for many years.

Another type of cork decoy is made from composition cork slabs, an industrial product employed principally for refrigerator insulation. Being composed of chips it lacks tensile strength and requires the addition of a wooden bottom, nailed or pegged to the main material. Due to the binder it has a much deeper color than cork in the natural form. It comes, however, in uniform rectangular shape and thickness and is very easily worked. For decoy bodies a three inch thickness is usually employed. Another quality of composition cork, denser and of greater strength, does not require a bottom board but is still subject to breakage under hard usage.

Real natural cork, however, is a splendid material, particularly for Black Duck. For this species, it never requires painting and seems to last forever.

Another material, used to some extent in modern decoys, is Balsa wood, a very light weight product of South America, which has become known in this country only in recent years. Soft and pithy in structure, Balsa wood cannot be subjected to rough usage. Decoys made of it require special painting to prevent absorption of water and special ballasting to prevent their being too lively in the water. After several experiments in making decoys with this wood, I found it advisable to use a counter-sunk yellow pine keel the full length of the body. This keel, about one inch deep and one and one-half inches wide, was set flush with the bottom of the decoy and pinned to the Balsa wood with wooden pegs set at a slight pitch. The head was made of white pine, secured to the body by a dowel three-eighths inch in diameter which extended downward through the keel. The keel thus added the necessary weight to the Balsa wood hull, gave a proper seat for the head dowel and furnished a solid fastening for anchor strap and weight. However, it should be noted, so much work is required to overcome the disadvantageous characteristics of Balsa wood, that its practicability is limited. Yet, with careful handling and proper care, it is well adapted for light duty decoys for use in shoal and sheltered waters.

XIII

Hollow Decoys

B Y WAY OF GENERAL DEFINITION, hollow decoys of the handmade type are built up of separate pieces of wood hollowed
out and subsequently fastened together. According to the best
available evidence, they made their appearance long after
solid decoys had been in general use. This later appearance
would appear quite normal since the construction is more
highly specialized.

Hollow decoys reached a stage of perfected development
in the decade following the Civil War. This fact is evidenced
by an account of decoy making which appeared in the year
1874. This printed reference occurs in a chapter devoted to
decoys, in Long's *American Wild-Fowl Shooting.** Though
published many years ago, Mr. Long's instructions are singu-
larly informing. Owing to the lack of similar data, I quote at
length from his remarks:

"One of the most important requisites, to insure success in
wild-fowl shooting, and more especially in the pursuit of deep
water variety is a suitable flock of decoys. They may be made in
a multitude of ways, and of several different materials, each of
which has its peculiar advantages, but at the same time its corresponding defects. The principal objects to be obtained by all, however, are naturalness, or a sufficient resemblance to the species they
are intended to represent, with the proper shape necessary to enable

*Joseph W. Long, "American Wild-Fowl Shooting." Published in New York, 1874.

[78]

PLATE 55
DOWITCHER *by Elmer Crowell*
East Harwich, Mass., about 1890

PLATE 56
BLACK–BREASTED PLOVER
Lawrence, L. I.

PLATE 57
DECOYS BY MASON (Left) AND STEVENS (Right) FACTORIES

PLATE 58
ROBIN SNIPE AND YELLOWLEGS
Tin Folding Decoys, Patented 1874

them to ride in an erect position during the heavy blows they are often exposed to. This last desideratum is often partially and, I might say, entirely overlooked in the desire to make the decoys as light as possible, and of such shape as to take the least room in transportation, with such objects in view, would-be inventors have tried a variety of methods in making them, and though certainly accomplishing their object in this respect, have failed most decidedly in the main thing needed.

"Decoys made of wood (not the things one usually finds in the gun shops, where they should be allowed to remain, but as constructed to use, according to reason and with the proper appreciation of the thing needed), are preferable to any others. Having had some little experience in their manufacture, as well as their use, and having the satisfaction of seeing my own used as models by better hunters, I will describe them as I think they should be made; willing at the same time to yield due deference to the opinion of others.

"My principal object has been to secure the best shape possible to prevent rolling, and to ensure with least extra weight an upright position at all times when in use. How I have endeavored to do this will be better understood from the annexed cuts, representing outlines of the decoy, than by any explanation I could convey in words. [See Plate No. 46.]

"White cedar and soft pine are undoubtedly the best wood for decoys, on account both of their extreme lightness and ease in cutting. Pine perhaps is better for heads, being less easily broken, while cedar is the most durable. The timber should be well seasoned and free from knots and sap. For ducks, two by six inches is the proper size, but for geese, larger timber is needed.

"The timber, being planed on one side and sawed in proper lengths, is next cut around on its edge, according to a pattern representing a horizontal section of the decoy intended. Two pieces are needed for each decoy, which must be gouged out to the proper thickness, thus making the decoy hollow. The head (which has been previously shaped) is fitted and fastened to the top part by a screw from beneath and the two parts being roughly hewed into shape in conformation with a side pattern, are, after being nicely fitted, glued or otherwise cemented firmly together, and the decoy rounded and finished smooth. After being thoroughly sand-papered, it should be wet slightly all over so as to raise the grain of the wood, and when dry should be again sand-papered. If the decoy be washed over with a thin dressing of shellac, it will prove much more impervious to water. This should be done before painting, and no varnish should be put on afterwards, as it makes the decoy too glaring when in the sun. When thoroughly smooth, a heavy coat of priming should be put on, of some neutral tint that will not show too plainly through the coloring coat; all of which should be mixed with raw oil, and without an artificial drier. The priming should be allowed to harden thoroughly before the colors are put on. No priming is used on many of the decoys for sale in the gun shops; consequently, they soon become water soaked and heavy, and the colors indistinct. Artists' tube colors should be used, being more lively and durable than common paint, and costing but little more; and the nearer the painting resembles the coloring of the natural duck the better. A small brass wire staple or piece of leather is to be fastened to the lower part of the breast, to attach the line to. A piece of lead, about four ounces in weight, formed as shown in the figure, should next be screwed onto the bottom lengthwise, and like a keel, and the decoy is complete.

"For shoal-water duck shooting, flat bottom, hollow decoys, of two and one-half inches in thickness, answer fully as well, as the water is seldom rough.

"Each decoy should be provided with a separate line and anchor, which last should be of lead, if convenient, as it is less liable to scratch the paint from decoys than anything else. This need never exceed four ounces in weight. The line should be what is known as "sixteen thread" seine twine, about one-tenth inch thick, of a length adapted to the depth of water, and attached to the staple or leather in the breast of the decoy. Instead of winding the line around the neck of the decoy, as is often done, the proper way is to wind it tightly around the middle, which may be done in much less time, an item of importance when taking up decoys in a heavy wind. And in setting them out again, instead of unwinding them turn by turn, the decoy should be taken by the head in one hand, and the lead thrown with the other to the place desired, the turns coming off towards the tail as the lead is thrown. A large flock of decoys may be set out in this way in a remarkably short time."

In connection with these remarks printed sixty years ago, this sportsman author has described decoys of the highest type of construction. Avoiding details, even species, he has confined himself to principle. A study of his instructions will show sound judgment and knowledge well expressed.

To continue the subject of hollow decoys and to show that Mr. Long was not alone in his fastidious decoy making at this period, I will call attention to other and contemporary hollow decoys of this type made at Stratford, Connecticut, as early as 1876.

Stratford decoys were uniformly fine, both in construction and portraiture and designed for use on the extensive marshes at the mouth of the Housatonic River. The material used was native white pine. Bodies were worked from material about three inches thick, first shaped, then hollowed out and finished with a copper fastened bottom board about one-half an inch thick. In hollowing out the bodies the main portions to be removed were bored by closely spaced auger holes, later to be carefully cleaned out with a gouge. The heads were fastened from the underside, as described by Long.

The Stratford makers had strongly marked conventions with respect to the shape of their bodies. The overhang breast was one of these, designed to over-ride the slush ice which swept down the river during both spring and fall shooting. Heads were uniformly low and beautifully carved. An equal amount of attention strangely enough, was directed to the tail. Here also the diagrammatic portraiture of species was continued.

The same careful attention was carried out in finishing. In the hands of the Stratford makers the painting of decoy plumage was an art. Black Duck and Blue-bill seemed a specialty. In Black Duck the fine marking of the head was carried out in great detail, also the indication of the deep, rich feathering of the body. The quiet penciled marking of the Blue-bill was reproduced by a graining comb, working through one color to another underneath. The accompanying illustrations show, much more clearly than words, the many fine characteristics of this locality. See Plate No. 47.

Contemporary with the Stratford decoys just discussed, were the equally perfect "Dug-outs" of the New Jersey coast. They differ from the Connecticut make in one notable characteristic—the bodies are smaller and heads somewhat over size. The reason for this disproportion in design is due to local conditions.

The gunning on the Jersey shore, from Bay Head down through Barnegat Bay is generally conducted in the so-called Barnegat Sneak Box as mentioned in chapter on Market Gunning.* In former days the whole rig was rowed or sailed to the gunning grounds by one man. At two dollars and fifty cents a day the old time guides handled the boat loaded with sportsmen, guns, shells and about 40 decoys. The customary rig had 24 Broad-bill, 6 Black Duck, 6 Brant and 6 Canada Geese.

The weight and size of decoys, therefore, were factors important in the operation of these local boats. As a result of this custom Jersey decoys became comparatively small and light in weight, but usually designed to ride high in the water and carry showy heads. The weights, usually made in the form of a flat lead pad, were also affected by the limitations of space. Even the larger goose decoys are ballasted in this fashion to facilitate stowing. (See Plate No. 98.)

The decoys shown in the accompanying plates are typical of the Barnegat region. Until recent years they were invariably made from white cedar saw-mill slabs. The local saw-mills furnished white cedar for the boat building industry so long associated with Barnegat, and from waste piles the local decoy maker obtained material for his decoys. The slabs were "free

---

* Barnegat Sneak Box, a broad beam, shallow skiff from twelve to fourteen feet long and often provided with a centre-board. The bottom has a convex section and the deck rises from slightly above the water line, thus showing a minimum of free-board. The deck is also convex having small cockpit and combing. Decoys are carried on deck, stowed in racks provided at the stern.

for the hauling." But today "waste piles" of such valuable material no longer exist; local white cedar swamps have been deforested, and except for certain minor needs, the decoy maker must buy his material on a commercial basis.

The waste slabs of varying thicknesses were, of course, flat on one side and rounded on the other. By joining two sections of slab with their flat sides together, the body of a decoy was half made, so to speak, without even the clip of an axe. The larger slabs from butt logs were used for making the bodies of Geese and Brant; the smaller for Broad-bill, Redhead and other species of ducks and snipe.

The process of making was as follows: The maker first marked out his body pattern on the flat sides of suitable sections of slabs and hewed them roughly to shape. When a sufficient number of these were hewn, he proceeded to dress the flat sides to a perfectly fair surface with a long smoothing plane. This done, the top and bottom pieces were pegged together with cedar dowels. At this stage of his operations each roughly formed body was marked by a saw cut directly back of the head location to the low point of the finished back. Since both top and bottom sections had, in a previous operation, been hewed to form, the work of shaping the bodies by means of a draw-knife or spoke-shave, was guided by the exact outlines of the horizontal sections. The work of shaping done, the two halves of the body were knocked apart and hollowed out. The thickness of material left for the walls of the decoys was about one-half inch with proper bearing surfaces being allowed for the fastening of the sections together. This fastening was accomplished by means of copper or galvanized iron nails, and the joints caulked as in boat building. The heads were also made of white cedar and after the usual fashion. The material was marked out on the wood from the maker's pattern, sawed on a band-saw if such was available, roughed out with a narrow-bladed draw-knife, and finished by means of a jack-knife.

The Barnegat makers rarely primed the whole decoy with

one general color. The general procedure of painting required two operations, the work of painting the body coming first. With the dry head as a hand-hold, the painter completed the plumage on the body by laying on each section of the desired pattern—all in one operation. The edges of the different tints could thus be wiped together, giving the effect of a softer and more natural appearance. By a second operation, and after the body painting was thoroughly dry, he painted the head in like manner, wet, with the colors wiped together.

Such was the fashion of making Barnegat decoys by contemporaries of Mr. Long, whose description of decoy making was given in the opening pages of this chapter. Such decoys have proved their practical value for many years in the duck shooting of the Jersey waters.

In localities other than the Connecticut shore and Barnegat, hollow decoys have not been generally employed. They are comparatively expensive and will not stand the rough handling that decoys are subject to. Under certain conditions, however, they are of proved worth and properly constructed will give long service. In another chapter I will deal with hollow decoys for special use on other waters.

XIV

Snipe Decoys

T HE PRINCIPLE on which snipe decoys are made is the oldest type of construction employed in the making of American decoys. The Lovelock Cave lures prove that. Heads of ducks and geese mounted on rush forms go back many centuries, but for the water birds the idea has been outmoded. Profile or stick-up decoys are still employed in the gunning of Canada Geese, but that is all. The custom survives chiefly in the making of snipe decoys.

The term "snipe decoy" is rather a general one and applied to all those species of shore birds which may be "whistled in" to a group of decoys and thus within gunshot. After the fashion of duck decoys, they simulate the birds, are commonly made of wood and supported by a leg-like stick tenoned in the body.

The original or emergency devices for decoying snipe and other susceptible shore birds almost defy description. They consisted of any convenient object that would resemble a long legged bird feeding on the ground. A bunch of grass or a clam shell supported by a cleft stick stuck up on the beach constituted such a device; so did a piece of cow dung set up in a short pasture. Freshly killed birds propped in position belong in the same category. Even in recent times, gunners without suitable decoys have enjoyed success with these crude substitutes.

WILD FOWL DECOYS

From such early and temporary devices, more permanent forms evolved. The first of these were of no particular species, made of wood, having flat bodies and usually unpainted. When real fancy, the gunners would obtain an effect of plumage by lashing or tacking wings of an actual bird to the flat sides. These decoys were later displaced by others having full body and painted plumage. In course of time several distinct species were adopted. Principal among these were Yellow-leg Snipe, Black-bellied Plover and Robin Snipe. In a lesser degree came Dowitcher, Sickle-billed Curlew and Hudsonian Curlew. In the usages of American fowling the names Snipe Decoys or Snipe Stool were used generally to cover the whole group. The making of these decoys, while not as exacting with respect to their requirements as the floating type, received very careful attention at the hands of the decoy makers on the Atlantic coast.

Although of less importance than duck shooting, the pursuit of shore birds in America had many followers. The snipe was a favorite quarry and "bay shooting" looked upon by many as a fascinating and "gentle sport." I am saying this in the past tense. Shore bird shooting is now prohibited due to the alarming scarcity of birds. At one period, extremely abundant, the whole family steadily lost ground; but there is good evidence that many species are once more increasing under the protection afforded them. They lack the stamina of wild ducks and seem bewildered by the advance of civilization. For the most part they are protected by a carefully observed closed season. The Wilson's or English Snipe is the only exception. He, alone, will lie to dogs. Strange to say he is the only shore bird not subject to attraction by decoys. Perhaps that saved him. Who knows?

While restrictions of present day duck shooting have greatly curtailed production, the making of duck decoys has never ceased. The continued closed season on shore birds, however, has completely stopped the making of snipe decoys. Let me

[86]

PLATE 59
ALUMINUM CASTING FROM A MAMMOTH CANVAS-BACK
by Mason Decoy Factory
About 1885

PLATE 60
MALE WIDGEON *by Stevens Decoy Factory*
About 1880

PLATE 61
WEIGHTS AND ANCHORS

show by a very old account, how snipe stool were used in the day of no restrictions. In 1856, Frank Forester, in his *Complete Manual,* makes the following observation on the subject of snipe shooting, as practiced at that time.*

"The mode of shooting these birds, is to lie concealed in boats, masked with sea trash and covered with reeds, on the edges of the hassocks where the snipes feed, in the small pools left among the grass by the receding tide. On the margin of these, the stools or decoys, admirable representations of the different species, carved in pine wood and painted so as to have deceived the unsuspicious eye of many a deluded greenhorn, are set up, and to them the passing flocks are whistled down by the surprising skill of the bayman, whose unerring sight instantly recognizes every species, by the motion of its wings, and the manner of its flight, when the birds are mere air drawn specks against the dusky, dawning sky; and whose imitative powers call it down by so perfect a simulation of its cry, that it rarely fails to answer and descend to the wily cheats which tempt it to destruction.

"To these decoys are added the killed birds as fast as they are gathered, which are propped up with sticks, after a manner peculiar to the amphibious human natives, so as to complete the mystification and delusion of the survivors."

Snipe decoys had been made and used by American fowlers long prior to this reference of Forester's; dating back in fact to the early years of the 19th century. In spite of this, there is little data on their history or development. Evolution can be indicated, however, by illustration of actual decoys arranged as far as possible in order of their years.

Plate No. 31, for example, shows an early shore bird decoy presented to the author by Mr. Eugene V. Connett. It comes from the South Shore of Long Island, birth place of many and varied fowling customs. In this decoy, no species is indicated, merely a slim necked bird with a long bill, to stand on a stick. Long ago it had been laid aside as a curio for when

* Frank Forester, "Complete Manual for Young Sportsmen," New York, 1856.

it came into my possession the flat left side bore an oblong of stained and aged paper bearing in faded ink this inscription:

Made about 1800 by
Ben Hawkins Bellport.
Shot over by four
generations of Hawkins.

The body of this decoy is roughly cut from white pine one-half inch in thickness. The head, neck and bill, in one piece, is made from a locust sapling and tenoned into the top edge of the body. The lower edge of the body has the customary hole for the leg or "stick." The present painting is faded to a sort of neutral brown. In places, however, this color is chipped away, showing an original tint of grey—undoubtedly intended for yellow-leg snipe. Authentic or not, that date of "about 1800" in faded ink, is the oldest claim encountered in connection with the history of snipe decoys.

Flat decoys of this type are unquestionably very old and were continued over a long period. Owing to extreme light weight, they were convenient to carry, thus practical for use in the field. Many of them were painted, others given an effect of plumage by the application of snipe wings to the flat sides. In this respect they recall the Indian use of feathers in lieu of paint.

From primitive but permanent lures such as these the making of snipe decoys moved slowly to a high degree of perfection. The next step may be illustrated by the Whittaker Snipe shown in Plate No. 52. These decoys were made in about 1850 by the late Captain John Whittaker, at that time owner of a hotel for sportsmen at Carnarsie, on the shore of Jamaica Bay. The bodies were hewn from round timber, again having heads and necks of natural locust. In these decoys it will be noted that a crude but effective painting of plumage is used.

From these forms which typify many observed examples, we pass to the third stage of construction employed in the making of shore bird decoys. In the later types it will be seen that body and head are carved from one piece of timber, white pine or white cedar. The bill, made of locust, white oak or other hard wood was tenoned into the head and fitted and shaped with great care. In fact, during the latter part of the 19th century, snipe decoys received more careful attention than duck decoys. The bodies were not only rounded to full form, but wing, tail and head were carved in true portraiture of species. The painting of shore bird decoys was also carried out in varying degrees of detail and excellence. The painting of snipe, however, presents many difficulties and few makers excelled in it. As in all decoy plumage the work was done in one operation with the colors worked together as in the process of painting a picture on canvas.

To show the degree of perfection to which snipe decoys were carried it gives me great pleasure to call attention to the Yellow-legs in Plate No. 53, and the Dowitcher in Plate No. 55. The first of these decoys was located on the Connecticut shore, the second in the rig of Mr. Frederick Becker of Long Island. Both were made about 40 years ago—perhaps earlier—but by one man, Mr. Elmer Crowell of East Harwich, Mass.

Mr. Crowell is a well known figure on Cape Cod, celebrated as a carver and painter of game birds. His present work is the direct outcome of many years spent in Massachusetts gunning and decoy making. In his work one finds a full expression of the American fowler's art.

Among the items of my collection are many fine shore birds but mostly of unknown origin. The Sickle-billed Curlew shown in Plate No. 114 is one of these—a gift of the late F. H. Stone of New York. It was found by Mr. Stone on Capers Island, off Charlestown, S. C. The body, hewn from round timber is nearly fourteen inches long. The present iron bill, while very old and pitted by the rust of years, is not original.

The group in Plate No. 54 gives several decoys from different localities. The Black-breasted plover loaned by Mr.

Frederick Becker, comes from Long Island, the Robin snipe from Chincoteague Island, Virginia. The Hudsonian Curlew with the iron bill and fine painting is Long Island again. The English wood pigeon at the bottom of plate comes from a firm of gun-smiths, of Birmingham, England—a modern and typical example of English decoy making. The decoy at the upper right, a Yellow-leg, shows an unusual type of construction from Nantucket Island. This last decoy is an interesting convention. The original owner, Mr. Bassett Jones of New York, could give no details as to age or maker—it was found in a Nantucket boat-house—that's all.

Occasionally, however, one encounters items of authentic snipe stool history. The long slim Yellow-legs of Plate No. 53, for example, is the work of the late Frank Kellum of Babylon, L. I. This man was one of the celebrated makers of his locality. Stories are still told of the skill and rapidity with which he made and painted decoys. He appears to have been a natural and gifted artist. All his work shows strong characteristics, great ease and knowledge. The decoy shown is reproduced through the courtesy of Mr. Percy Cushing.

The subject of snipe decoys is difficult to terminate. Were the space available, I would show pictures and tell the story of every shore bird I own or have in my possession. I say possession because in some cases my title of ownership is not exactly clear. That Yellow-leg, for instance, is being held pending notice from Mr. Cushing to return. The same holds good for other decoys I like to think of as my own. But somehow I have come to believe that few of these "loans" will ever be called in. To hear a boy practising the plaintive call of snipe seems definitely a thing of the past. I know of but one "silver whistle" still in existence. I have seen no shore bird decoys in process of making for several years. Perhaps they will never be made again. Bay shooting seems remote and I look upon my old snipe decoys, title or no title, with affection; historical fragments of American wild fowl history.

PLATE 62
CAST-IRON BROADBILL
Great South Bay, L. I., about 1885

PLATE 64
CAST-IRON CANVAS-BACK
Havre de Grace, Md.

PLATE 63
CAST-IRON RUDDY DUCK
Back Bay, Va.

XV

Factory Decoys

While the so-called "Gun Store" decoy lacked the quality of those made by hand, it is obvious that the machine made article is entitled to a place in the records of American wild fowling. They were sufficient to the needs of many duck shooters. Upon examination it will also be found that the introduction of machinery exerted a strong influence in the standardization of decoys.

The making of decoys by machinery had its beginning in the years following the Civil War. The new product immediately became known as the factory decoy. Decoy factories were never numerous but a few concerns continued production over many years. Strange to say the earliest and most important of these were not established near coastal gunning grounds, but made their appearance in the Middle West. Among the earliest of them were the Dodge factory and the Mason factory, both of Detroit, Michigan. Why Detroit should become a decoy headquarters is not clear. It may have been due, however, to the rapid development of a new country abounding in game and the increasing demand of the wild fowl markets. A third concern of importance was the Stevens factory located at Weedsport, New York.

For many years previous to the enactment prohibiting the sale of game, these and lesser known concerns made and sold thousands of decoys annually. There were grades and classification with respect to design, size and quality: solid decoys, hollow decoys, large and small decoys; with glass eyes and those with tack eyes, etc. Plumage patterns of both male and female were elaborately painted, and for the most part factory decoys both good and bad were fitted with naturalistic glass eyes.

Packed in barrels or crates, this singular embodiment of the growing machine age, were shipped to gunning grounds throughout the country. Prices ranged from $2.50 per dozen up to $9.00 and even $12.00 per dozen. A fair percentage of them were of good design and workmanship; yet as a whole, factory decoys were never accepted in certain localities. Generally speaking, the more discriminating gunners of the Atlantic coast, even up to the close of market shooting and after, preferred to use handmade decoys. The factories, however, sold to Southern and Western States in almost unbelievable quantities and for this reason played an important part in the history of duck shooting. What machines lacked in quality was made up in quantity and helped to standardize the tools of a growing trade.

Early manufacturing methods were very simple. For the most part, bodies were turned in a reproducing lathe, a type of machine in which the tool work is automatically guided by a model made of hard wood or iron. Due to limitations of the machine, breast and tail were finished by hand. The making of heads required even a greater amount of hand work, but the process resulted in decoys of uniform size and shape, predetermined by the model employed.

While there were other pioneer producers of machine-made decoys, it will serve our purpose here to consider the factories already mentioned. All three were conducted along similar lines at the beginning and all have now ceased production. Their influence, however, is still apparent in their products recalled by many contemporary, but older, sportsmen.

Decoy factories seem to have been of too lowly a character

to have warranted the attention of historians. Information about the Dodge decoy factory of Detroit was gained by chance but is of sufficient interest to warrant the following record. In 1921, while located in Rochester, an account of my decoy collection was published as a news item in the Rochester *Herald*. The story itself is not important but it brought about an interesting interview. A few days after the appearance of the story I received a visit from a Mr. Dodge, an older man, then a member of the faculty of the University of Rochester. After introductions were over he explained his visit; he had come for the purpose of seeing some old decoys.

It appeared that as a boy he had been employed to apply glass eyes in the heads of decoy ducks. It was his first job after leaving school, in his father's back-yard factory on the outskirts of Detroit. His father, as a young man, worked in a Detroit gun store, and becoming aware of the growing market for decoys, had bought a second-hand lathe from a German shoemaker who also made shoe lasts, and started the J. M. Dodge factory, in 1867–69. There may have been earlier decoy factories, but if so I am unaware of them. I regret that I am unable to reproduce an example of a Dodge decoy.

But that is not the end of this unexpected and unsolicited story. Shortly after Mr. Dodge's father had turned his attention to the manufacture of decoys by machinery, another young man of Detroit appeared one day at the gun store, with a Mallard drake which he himself had made. It was very finely modeled and painted, Mr. Dodge assured me, far superior to any decoy his father made, or had ever seen. This young man with the "beautiful Mallard," subsequently became a rival of his father, founding the Mason decoy factory of Detroit.

In after years, Mason decoys became the most widely known of all decoys made by machinery. It was a well made product and for that period well advertised. The Mason line covered many species, all of marked and consistent design. On Plate No. 57 I show a female Mallard, one of the standard models; on Plate No. 59 what was designated as the Mammoth Canvas-back. This decoy curiously enough is an aluminum casting from one of the original decoys.

Last but not least of the pioneers came the Stevens decoy factory located at Weedsport, New York, a small village in the vicinity of the Montezuma Marshes. This region, lying between Lake Ontario on the north and the Finger Lakes on the south, was at one time a celebrated gunning ground. The Montezuma has since been drained, but here in an old time paradise of waterfowl, the Stevens factory made some of the finest decoys ever produced by machinery. In Plate No. 57 I show two of them, the Whistler at the upper right was found on the shore of Oneida Lake—to be exact, in my grandfather's barn. It belonged to my father and dates back to the 'eighties. The little Buffle-head at the lower right was a present from my brother Lyman, and is, without doubt, of the same period. Plate No. 60 shows a Stevens Widgeon which the late Herman Stone found among the old decoys of the Currituck Club in North Carolina. In this decoy the painting is original and still shows the work of a "graining comb" on the back.

The "tin snipe" in Plate No. 58 shows a patented design placed on the market in 1874. This device made of pressed tin, was very popular and used in great numbers; one of the best "gunstore decoys" of the period. They were composed of two halves, hinged at the top and held together by a ferrule on the end of the supporting stick. By removing the stick, the halves could be opened and many decoys nested together in a very compact space.

But all of these old concerns have now left the field of production. Under post-war conditions they were unable to survive. Their chief support had been taken away by the Federal restrictions of 1913–1918. A few years after the war, the Mason factory issued catalogues and resumed manufacture, but after a single season withdrew again. Subsequently several new manufacturers have attacked the problem but none of

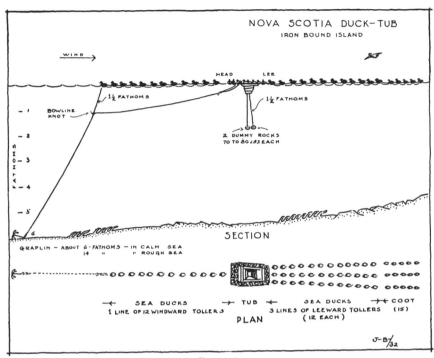

PLATE 65

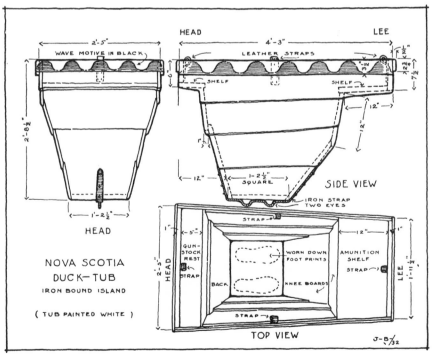

PLATE 66

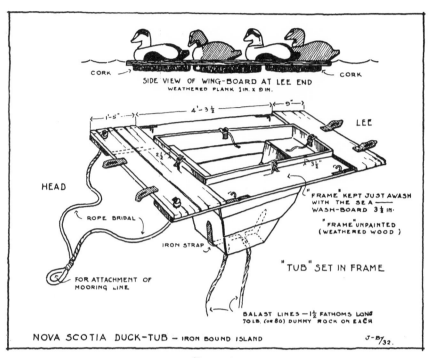

CORK — SIDE VIEW OF WING-BOARD AT LEE END — CORK
WEATHERED PLANK 1 IN. X 9 IN.

LEE

1'-5"   4'-3½"   9"

HEAD

2½"   3½"

ROPE BRIDAL

"FRAME" KEPT JUST AWASH
WITH THE SEA
WASH-BOARD 3½ IN.

"FRAME" UNPAINTED
(WEATHERED WOOD)

IRON STRAP

"TUB" SET IN FRAME

FOR ATTACHMENT OF
MOORING LINE

BALAST LINES — 1½ FATHOMS LONG
70 LB. (OR 80) DUMMY ROCK ON EACH

NOVA SCOTIA DUCK-TUB — IRON BOUND ISLAND   J-B/32.

PLATE 67

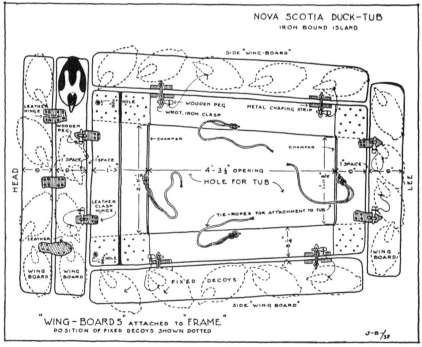

NOVA SCOTIA DUCK-TUB
IRON BOUND ISLAND

SIDE "WING-BOARD"

LEATHER
HINGE

WOODEN PEG
WROT. IRON CLASP

METAL CHAPING STRIP

WOODEN
PEG

CHAMFER   CHAMFER

HEAD

1 SPACE   1 SPACE

9"   9"   1'-5"

LEE

4'-3½" OPENING

HOLE FOR TUB

1 SPACE

9"   9"

LEATHER
CLASP
HINGE

TIE-ROPES FOR ATTACHMENT TO TUB

LEATHER

WING
BOARD

WING
BOARD   WING
BOARD

FIXED DECOYS

SIDE "WING BOARD"

"WING-BOARDS" ATTACHED TO "FRAME"
POSITION OF FIXED DECOYS SHOWN DOTTED

J-B/32

PLATE 68

them with the vigor and success of their predecessors. Something is amiss.

But decoys are still required by duck shooters, and, if I may prophesy, the needs of the future will be met, not by hand makers but by machines. This coming era will employ new methods and carving machines. The new decoys will be better designed than ever before, made of the best material with well-studied painting of plumage. These decoys will move into the hands of the American sportsman, really a very fastidious person, who will pay the price imposed by new conditions. When this time comes, decoys, like guns, will be passed along to sportsmen's sons, and thus become gunning heirlooms.

XVI

Weights and Anchors

ALTHOUGH REFERENCE has been made in preceding chapters to the rigging of decoys, the subject is of sufficient importance to justify a summary chapter. To be serviceable, a decoy must be provided with a suitable anchor and be so ballasted as to remain upright and ride properly under all conditions. To illustrate the variety of these accessories, I append Plate No. 61 for reference.

The ballast or "weight" is fashioned in many ways; very many. A railroad spike, attached to the bottom of a decoy will serve as ballast, but in carefully equipped decoys, various standard and accepted shapes are used. In the early days weights were commonly made of iron. Lead, however, is a far superior material as it will not mar the painting of other decoys with which it may come in contact.

On the shores of Barnegat Bay the customary method of ballasting decoys is to apply a thin lead pad, not more than a quarter inch in thickness and secured to the bottom by means of small brass screws. For duck decoys these pads vary from 2½ to 3 inches square; for brant and geese, larger as required. In some cases these squares are solid castings, in others built up in sheets to the required thickness. In all cases, edges are worked off to eliminate sharp angles or corners. These weights answer very well for the light hollow decoys of this region

PLATE 69
MALE EIDER DUCK *by Capt. Harris Young*
Ironbound Island, Nova Scotia, about 1920

PLATE 70
FEMALE EIDER DUCK *by Capt. Harris Young*
Ironbound Island, Nova Scotia, about 1920

PLATE 71
LOON *by Albert Orme*
Southport, Me., about 1875

PLATE 72
NEW ENGLAND COOTING DORY

and their compactness facilitates storing of the decoys in the limited space provided in the typical Barnegat boats.

In the Chesapeake Bay region, particularly on the Susquehanna Flats, another type of weight has been developed to meet the requirements imposed by local conditions. The decoys of this locality are usually of the solid type and the regulation weights are in the form of a lead or iron keel about four inches long. This keel is necessarily placed well aft on the center line of the decoy as shown in the contemporary Canvas-back decoy in Plate No. 102. It thus serves as ballast and also helps the decoy to ride properly at anchor. Early keels of this type were made of iron with staple-like ends to be driven into the body of the decoy. (See Fig. 3 in Plate No. 61.) In later years, however, owing to its superior qualities, lead has become the accepted material. In making lead keels, bars of about ½ inch square section are cut to proper lengths and the ends flattened. They are made fast to the body by means of copper nails driven through the flattened ends.

Another Chesapeake keel, used lower down on the Eastern Shore of Maryland, consists of an iron horse-shoe, or rather a mule shoe as illustrated in Fig. 15. In this instance the iron shoe is cut in half, and the curved end forged to a sharp point to permit of being driven into the body, a very simple and effective keel.

Another standard body weight is the solid lead casting of pear-shape design which is used on the Connecticut shore. (See Fig. 2.) For duck decoys, this device is about ½ inch thick and 2½ inches long. The width at the wider end is about 1¼ inches and tapers forward to a rounded point. It is located on the center line of the decoy and secured by a single screw passing through the wider end of the weight. If the decoy lists, the point may be swung out in such a fashion as to overcome the lack of balance.

On the Great South Bay several types of body weights are used. Modifications of both keel and pad seem equally popular but neither may be considered a standard. This region, however, has one device for ballasting decoys, which is not used elsewhere and deserving of attention. This consists of a swinging weight suspended from the bottom of the decoy. The weights themselves vary; a few links of iron chain are frequently employed as in Fig. 4, a lead cylinder of about ¾ inch suspended by a wire shank is another form (see Fig. 5), and equally popular is a short piece of ⅝ inch iron rod with an eye at the upper and flattened end. These hanging weights are attached to the bottom of the decoy by an iron staple to permit them to swing freely. While effective in balancing the decoy, this weight has serious drawbacks; it is a hindrance in stowing, and is likely to cause fouling of the anchor lines. In my opinion it was originally devised as a means of overcoming hurriedly made and badly balanced decoys. A stool, even on its back, is instantly righted by the swinging action of this ballast as the decoy rolls in the sea. They were employed principally on the rough and ready decoys of the old South Bay battery rigs. I have never seen them used elsewhere. Many old decoys in this region still carry them.

In the Back Bay region of Virginia and upper Currituck Sound another standard weight is found. This consists of an iron casting, shaped as shown in Fig. 6. These weights are about 3 inches long, 1 inch wide and weigh from 8 to 12 ounces. The lower part of the casting is curved as shown in the illustration. It is fastened to the bottom of the decoy by means of screws set through holes provided in ends. An example is shown on the oversize Canvas-back in Plate No. 3.

One more decoy weight of special interest is the device illustrated in Fig. 16. In this type three bead-like lead weights are suspended from the bottom of the decoy on a short length of ¼ inch manila line secured to the wood by iron staples. Unlike the keel form, it is rigged athwart-wise of the decoy. The beads are free on the line and automatically adjust themselves to the center. The examples illustrated weigh 4 ounces each, making a total ballast of 12 ounces. The rig illustrated is typical of many coot decoys in the vicinity of Gloucester and Annisquam, Massachusetts.

The anchors used in the mooring of decoys vary greatly in design. There are certain standard types, however, which have been universally used over a long period and these I will describe. Principal among the standard shapes is the truncated pyramid and truncated cone of lead or iron and provided with a ring or eye at the top for attachment of the mooring line. These pyramid or cone anchors vary in weight from 6 to 16 ounces for duck decoys, proportionately heavier for brant and geese. The gunners of the Susquehanna Flats commonly used the truncated pyramid type, but the pyramid is hollow, having walls of cast iron, and provided with a crude swivel of heavy copper wire for the anchor line fastening. In these iron anchors, all sharp corners are rounded off to prevent marring the painting of other decoys with which they may come in contact. These anchors, chiefly employed for solid decoys in the gunning of Canvas-back, weigh 16 ounces. (See Fig. 12.)

Another design popular on the Chesapeake consists of a cast lead triangle, having sides of about 3 inches, base about 2½ inches and ½ inch in thickness. The example shown in Fig. 1 comes from North East, Maryland, and weighs 16 ounces. It is typical of those used for mooring Canvas-back decoys with 10 to 12 foot anchor line. Both pyramid and triangle types have a distinct advantage in the process of taking up. Grass and mud will not adhere to the sloping sides upon coming aboard the boat.

Another type of mooring widely used and popular in many localities is the "mushroom" anchor. To the best of my belief the mushroom was originally introduced by decoy factories. It consists of a saucer-like lead weight provided with a wire shank as shown in Fig. 8. The popular weight is 8 ounces. The merits of "mushroom" are rather patent. I will call attention, therefore, to its less obvious drawbacks. The saucer-like weight not only buries itself in soft bottoms, but on coming aboard brings with it objectionable quantities of mud and grass. For this reason their early popularity has waned. For shoal water uses, however, they are still considered practical.

An improvement on the wire shanked mushroom was subsequently introduced by practical gunners to be used principally for mooring geese decoys. These new mushrooms, including the shank or standing part, were cast in solid lead. In this type the base of the shank curved outward to the rim of saucer. While these anchors proved as tenacious as the earlier forms, they had the merit of clearing themselves when pulled through the water. Grass and other foreign matter would not adhere to the sloping sides of the shank.

In recent years decoy anchors in the form of lead or iron rings have steadily gained in favor. The closed horse-shoe shown in Fig. 7 is probably the first expression of the idea. The horse-shoe anchor was introduced by battery gunners of the Great South Bay. Local blacksmiths joined the open ends of discarded shoes, thus forming an iron ring of proper weight which could be dropped over the head of the decoy when not in use. In the process of forging the ring, the worn out calks of the shoes were hammered out. The resulting anchor was cheap and effective. Since battery shooting requires the use of many anchors, the horse-shoe was very popular and rightly so. In picking-up, the ring is dropped over the head of the decoy, eliminating the possibility of fouling anchor lines while in process of stowing.

This crude device was undoubtedly the forerunner of the lead rings used extensively and for many years on the shore of Connecticut. Modern batteries on the Great South Bay now also employ lead rings, round or oval castings weighing about 16 ounces having an interior dimension of about $3\frac{1}{2}$ inches to permit of passing over the decoy's head. A still later development is the commercial anchor shown in Fig. 13. In this type

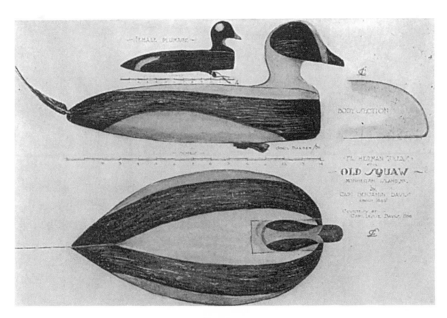

PLATE 73
OLD SQUAW *by Capt. Benjamin Davis*
Monhegan Island, Me., 1865

PLATE 74
MALE EIDER DUCK
Monhegan Island, Maine

PLATE 75
WHITE-WINGED COOT
Monhegan Island, Maine

PLATE 76
COOT SHADOW DECOYS
Cape Ann, Mass., 1870

the ring is provided with projections which form a reel for the anchor line. The weight of this anchor is 16 ounces. When not in use the line is not wound on the body of the decoy but on the reel.

In using the plain ring anchors, the line is wound around the body of the decoy, and in setting out decoys so rigged, the anchor is lifted off the head and thrown into position by the right hand while, simultaneously, the decoy is thrown into position with the left, the turns of the line coming off the body before the latter strikes the water. In setting out decoys rigged with the reel type of ring, a few turns of line are released from the reel and the anchor and decoy thrown into position together. As the anchor sinks in the water, the turns come free and the pull of the decoy establishes the length of line required.

Figure 10 shows a commercial anchor combining the features of both ring and mushroom. It is very effective as a mooring but has the drawback of the original wire-shanked mushroom. Yet for many purposes it is practical and convenient.

When mooring a trawl line of sea duck decoys, in water depths of from 3 to 6 fathoms, nothing can compare in effectiveness with a 5 pronged "graplin" (grapnel). From Long Island Sound to ocean shoals off the coast of Nova Scotia, the use of this wrought-iron contrivance of shank and hooks is universal. It will "grapple" and hold on the hardest bottom and is light in weight. For mooring a heavy trawl on ledges, it has no equal.*

The weights described in the first part of this chapter had to do with the balancing of decoys. There are other "weights" used by duck shooters, a peculiar form of ballast and deserving of record here. These weights are the heavy cast-iron decoys employed as ballast on the deck of the sink box or battery. On the platform of these submerged boxes, from 6 to 8 iron decoys are required to "sink" the deck and wings to as near the level

*See Chapter XVII, Nova Scotia decoys.

of the water as possible. Originally the decoys set on the decks of batteries were for the purpose of screening the gunner only. At this stage they were made of wood and spiked to the deck. The use of wooden ducks for this purpose is illustrated in Plate No. 68 showing the Nova Scotia Duck Tub. An old-time wing-duck from Elkton, Maryland, is shown in Plate No. 12.

Due, however, to the necessity of adjusting ballast to meet varying conditions, deck decoys are now commonly made of cast-iron. The first of these weights was made by using a standard full-bodied decoy as a model for casting. The full-bodied casting, however, was too heavy to be practical. As a result of this the body was flattened to about 2 to $2\frac{1}{4}$ inches, giving an average weight of about 25 pounds per unit.

An example of the full-bodied cast-iron decoy is shown by the Great South Bay Broad-bill in Plate No. 62. It dates back to the 'eighties and weighs about 30 pounds. It carries also the old South Bay painting for the drake decoy of this species. Plate No. 63 shows a full-bodied Ruddy Duck weight from Back Bay, Virginia, weight $20\frac{1}{2}$ pounds. The hole in the tail provides fastening for a line in case of the decoy going overboard.

The Canvas-back shown in Plate No. 64 comes from Havre de Grace, Maryland, and is typical of the weights used on the batteries of the Susquehanna Flats. It is a contemporary example, weighing 25 pounds. The chief variation in modern cast-iron decoys is found in the model itself. Some of them are very fine. The standard weight of 25 pounds, however, seldom varies.

PLATE 77
SLAT GOOSE AND MALE OLD SQUAW *by Joseph W. Lincoln*
Accord, Mass, 1931

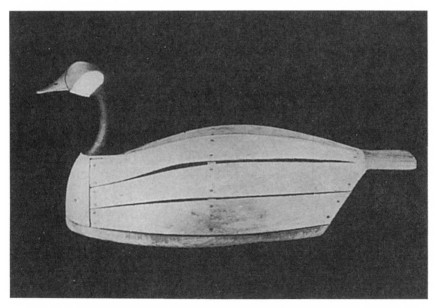

PLATE 78
CANVAS GOOSE FRAME *by Joseph W. Lincoln*
Accord, Mass., 1931

PLATE 79
SLEEPING BLUE-BILL *from rig of John C. Phillips*
Wenham, Mass., 1928

PLATE 80
CENTENNIAL BROADBILL *by Benjamin Holmes*
Stratford, Conn., 1876

PART VI

XVII

Regional Decoys

NOVA SCOTIA

THE PURPOSE OF THIS BOOK is centered on decoys and decoy history. It is not intended to cover forms of duck shooting or necessarily the ways in which decoys are used. But collecting decoys has brought to light phases of American gunning that transcend decoys yet are closely related. The "duck tub" of Nova Scotia is one of these items; even a decoy book cannot afford to pass it by.

To the best of my belief, no printed reports of this particular ducking machine have ever appeared. I have never been aboard one of these "tubs," but to the battery gunners of the Middle and Southern Atlantics, the details of method and operation should be a source of inspiration if not envy. It is for this reason that I digress and tell the story of North Atlantic duck shooting as practiced by fishermen off the coast of Nova Scotia, particularly by those intrepid gunners of Ironbound Island.

The postoffice of Ironbound is Blanford, a village on the main land between Mahone Bay and St. Margaret Bay. The island lies about ten miles out to sea. The land area is small— not to exceed a hundred acres. Inhabitants are confined to but three principal families. It is a small world of sea activities. The men are fishermen who follow the water from one year's end to another. On the landward side is the cove, with a strip of beach to serve the dories. The cove is too small to afford shelter but has a mooring for the convenience of visitors. At nightfall, all boats, both large and small, are hauled clear of the sea and tide—come high water.

Visitors to Ironbound are rare.

Occasionally an artist, sometimes two or three will spend the summer there, painting the rocks and sea. But as August draws to a close, there are goodbyes and departure. With the coming of cold weather, however, new pilgrims appear, not to the island this time, but far off shore on outlying shoals. The newcomers are ducks, sea ducks and in great numbers. They lie on shoals and dive for mussels; big black Coot, parti-colored Old Squaw and lastly Eider Duck. The Eider, who lives always at sea, is nearing the end of his migratory range and is inclined to tarry here for the winter.

Viewed from the cliffs the visitors present a picture of singular fascination, particularly the Eiders. The huge black and white drakes in company with sombre mates and pinto offspring are indications of future feather beds and a change of diet. But the birds lie in treacherous and open water, protected by inaccessibility of their own making. And what protection! They are ten miles out in the ocean, living and feeding in from six to fourteen fathoms of water. The method employed in gunning them to me seems heroic. So much so that in the summer of 1930, I commissioned a friend to diagram the rig and note the details of the system.*

In offering the material for publication, great care has been taken, not only to retain the facts but to convey the character and quality of the original notes. The diagrams have been remade for the purpose of reproduction, but are otherwise without change; the notes transcribed to follow a chronological order. The pictorial feature is of special interest. Coupled with completeness of detail, all diagrams were made under the direct supervision of Captain Harris Young of Ironbound,

* Mr. John McPherson, of New York.

PLATE *81*

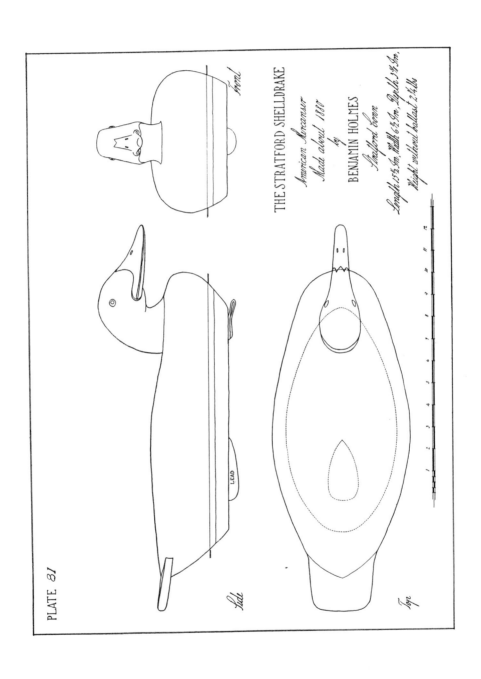

Front

THE STRATFORD SHELLDRAKE

American Merganser
Made about 1880
by
BENJAMIN HOLMES
Stratford Conn.

Length 15½ In., Width 6½ In., Depth 5½ In.
Weight without ballast 2¼ lbs

LEAD

Side

Top

PLATE 82
CANADA GOOSE *by Charles E. Wheeler*
Stratford, Conn., 1931

owner of the rig. Captain Young is acknowledged one of the most expert gunners on the coast and without his kindly assistance, the material could not have been assembled.

Reference to Plate No. 65 shows plan and sectional views of the complete rig, moored in the minimum water depth of six fathoms. The principal features are designated as follows— graplin anchor, mooring line, single line of windward tollers, box for the gunner with wing boards and carrying decoys for the purpose of screening the occupant, and finally the three lines of leeward tollers. In this plate, also, is shown the method of ballasting by means of rocks suspended on lines attached to the bottom of the box.

The entire rig, with all lines of tollers, pays out to leeward of the graplin, the gunner shooting to leeward as the birds come in against the wind. On the surface, the set is approximately 80 feet over all and include 78 Sea-duck decoys, supplemented by 15 Coot attached to the leeward lines. In the old days, the average number of decoys, or tollers so called, was somewhat greater. A similar rig twenty years ago would carry up to one hundred Sea-ducks with a proportionate increase in Coot.

To permit of transportation by dory, the tub is composed of separate and demountable units. To accomplish this feature and still be seaworthy seems a masterpiece of nautical ingenuity. To make this clear I will again refer to the diagrams.

Plate No. 66 shows side and end views of the tub from which the gunner kills his birds. While somewhat crude in appearance, the shape is carefully designed to conform to the crouching figure of a man. In the original notes, the long and continued use of this particular box is indicated by the following: "The bottom of the box is worn down to a depth of about one-half inch, in the shape of two extra large foot prints."

Plate No. 67 shows the tub and "Frame" joined together with the necessary deck fittings. This plate also details the mooring line bridle under the head of the frame and the wrought-iron fitting at the bottom of the box which carries the ballast ropes.

Plate No. 68 gives layout of wing boards on which depend the safety of the gunner. Here, also, are shown the various fittings for attachment to frame and location of decoys carried on deck. These wing decoys, which are necessary to screen the occupant, are spiked solidly in permanent arrangement. Additional buoyancy is obtained for the wings by the application of cork to the under side. These members, like the frame, are not painted but made of naturally weathered planks.

The trip to the gunning grounds and "the set" is made before daylight, the rig being handled by two men in a 16-foot dory. Tub and frame only are assembled before leaving the beach, all other paraphernalia is stowed loose in the order required when making the set.

Arrived at the shoal, the first consideration is proper anchorage. The location selected is always on the ocean side of the shoal. In a calm sea, a depth of about six fathoms is selected; a heavy sea calling for fourteen fathoms or more. The graplin set and the dory standing directly over, the trawl of twelve windward tollers is made fast to the mooring line. (See Plate No. 65.) The mooring line is then paid out, the dory falling off to leeward. When clear of the tollers, the end of the mooring is tied into the loop of the rope bridle under the head of the "frame." The dummy rocks attached to lines on the bottom of the box are then lowered over the side and the joined tub and frame thrown into the sea.

Still working from the dory, the crew next set the wing-boards in place and the box is complete. With the addition of wings, the tub is now ready to receive the occupant. The three lines of leeward tollers are paid out over the stern of the dory, and the gunner goes aboard to complete the remaining items. He first attaches the lines of leeward tollers to the necks of three special decoys spiked on the after wing-board; then, on the unoccupied frame around the box, arranges ten or fifteen loose rocks weighing about ten pounds each. This movable weight is required to ballast the frame down to the surface of the water. Finally, he places a few loose decoys on the frame to conceal the rocks.

Total number of tollers as follows:

12 on windward line
36 on three leeward lines
22 fixed on wing-boards
8 loose decoys on frame.

In the spring the decoys should include about fifty percent white and black drakes and fifty percent grey brown ducks. Only a dozen white drakes should be used in the fall. At this season of the year, the grey or brown birds represent both ducks and young drakes—the latter being colored like the ducks, except white on the breast and minor variations, according to age. Also, after the mating season, the old drakes are inclined to travel by themselves, far out on the ocean shoals where it is safer. As a final illustration, I show pictures of two Ironbound tollers. (See Plates No. 69 and 70.) Through the courtesy of Captain Young, this Eider drake, together with the brown duck, was added to the author's collection of decoys.

But to resume the story of operation: with all gear set, the final items are taken on board and fixed in position. The shell box is placed on the ammunition shelf at the lee end, the gun stock supported on the smaller ledge at the head of the tub with barrels pointing to lee. In this position, there is less chance of water entering the barrels, should a sea break over the tub.

Thus equipped, the man in the tub squats down, his feet taking their place in the worn-down footprints of the bottom. He is now ready for the business of Sea-duck shooting. As day breaks over the Atlantic, the man in the dory rows off to leeward; his part being to pick up birds and watch his mate for signals.

This is the Ironbound duck tub. A reference to the Plates will disclose that the tub itself displaces less water than a standard size bath tub. It is so small that it fits the occupant like a strait-jacket. The life-giving wings are "awash," and the actual freeboard a matter of three and one-half inches. It is designed, however, to lie in heavy weather, ten miles out on the Atlantic, over six to fourteen fathoms of unsheltered water, and does—just that. The hinged wings, held awash by the heavy decoys, wring and follow the undulation of the waves; at the head of the box, the cork floats keep the gear well up, riding and flattening advancing seas. A comber may *break across* the tub but that is not serious; nor yet at the lee end where it only sweeps away the tollers on the after wing.

Sometimes when a dead calm occurs, the wash board of the tub "looms," causing the birds to sheer off and avoid the rig. When this transpires, rather than waste time signaling the dory, the gunner takes his bailer and fills the tub about one-third full of water, or up to his boot tops. By this procedure the box is again lowered out of sight.

When the man in the box wants the dory, either to pick up birds or to be taken up on account of the sea, he signals by waving his cap, or in rough weather, his oil jacket. With only three inches of vertical wash board, his position looks very hazardous but the wings are always at work, flattening out seas and lifting the frame up to the larger wave planes before being tipped and submerged.

As a matter of fact, by fishermen it is not considered very dangerous, unless the wind starts to run crosswise over a strong tide or undertow. When this occurs, the wind lop, and swell movement form a dangerous chop. The man in the tub must then signal for his tender, cast out his movable rock ballast, and thus raise the deck an inch or two. The cork lining on the wings is also another saving factor. In case a wave does break

CORK BLACK DUCK   PLATE 83   CORK COOT
By Charles E. Wheeler
Stratford, Conn., 1931

FEMALE MALLARD   PLATE 84   MALE MALLARD
By Charles E. Wheeler
Stratford, Conn., 1931

FEMALE WHISTLER   PLATE 85   MALE WHISTLER
By Charles E. Wheeler
Stratford, Conn., 1931

MALE OLD SQUAW   PLATE 86   FEMALE OLD SQUAW
By Charles E. Wheeler
Stratford, Conn., 1931

over and fill the box, the buoyancy will keep the tub awash, giving a few moments to get bailed out. Ordinary quantities of bailing, or ice freezing about the boots and knees, are taken as a matter of course.

My object to describe the Nova Scotia Duck Tub seems now to have been accomplished. The adventure of killing Eider ducks from the device is still another story. In his handling of the original data, my friend J. McPherson was extremely matter-of-fact. Nowhere among his notes can be found an expression of wonder or admiration, either for the rig or the gunner. In view of this, I, too, will refrain from comment. I hope, however, that to some extent, the picture has been conveyed; that the reader can visualize that long line of tollers, rising and falling, appearing and disappearing, in the heavy seas off Ironbound. I trust, also, that the gear will always—"hold." I hope those magic wings will forever lift the intrepid island gunner out of danger; that the on-coming Atlantic will never come tragically aboard—at most, "only to carry away the tollers on the after wing, in its boiling wake."

Regional

UPPER COAST

My friend McPherson came back from Nova Scotia with information that island fishermen used Loon decoys. He even made a colored sketch of one but obtained no details as to how or why they were used. To a collector of the middle coast, a Loon decoy is something to puzzle about. Why a Loon anyway? But ultimately I learned the story and acquired an example; not from Nova Scotia but one that hailed from Southport, Maine.

I prize it highly. It came to light through persistent 'longshore inquiry and the kindness of Captain Ben Rand of Booth Bay Harbor. It had been made by a onetime light-house tender of Hendricks Head Light, Sheepscot Bay. His name was Albert Orme. When it came into my hands it still carried in turns around the body, six or eight fathoms of tarred line with a stone anchor attached. The ballast consisted of a second stone, secured to the flat bottom by leather straps. In spite of having been used over two generations the decoy was in fine condition, even the painting. The colors, being in black and white, are clearly shown in the accompanying photograph. (Plate No. 71.) I did not talk to the retired light-house tender —the story of how a Loon decoy is used was told by Captain Rand.

It is well known that a Loon is habitually solitary and extremely wary. To lure him to ambush seems beyond the range of credibility. But, gunners, listen to this. When a bird is sighted, no dory goes overboard or other activity is visible from the water. The whole performance is conducted from concealment among the rocks at the water's edge. The long anchor line coiled at his feet, the gunner quietly launches the decoy, paying out the line as the decoy is carried out on an ebbing tide. The anchor follows, cast to the limit of the mooring line beyond the decoy. When in final position, the toller is riding some twenty or thirty yards off the point.

His lure in position, the gunner then begins the "calling" process quite out of sight in his blind among the rocks. Curiosity aroused by the strange bird, and enticed by the skillful calling, the Loon slowly works in toward shore. He does this in a series of dives, each time approaching nearer. On the last dive he breaks water *in-shore* of the decoy Loon. But that is not all. Due to habitual caution, he comes up *facing seaward* . . . Wham!

After this the dory appears around the rocky point. Drifting out to sea rides the Loon—shot in the back. The man in the dory picks him up and then retrieves the decoy. The bleak monotony of Hendricks Head Light is broken. There is wild fowl in the larder.

"To cook a loon," says Captain Rand, "they parboil first and use some sort of 'chemical'; then they roast it."

Rather impressed by the word "chemical," the writer ventured the question—Soda?

"Maybe 'twas," said the Captain, "but if they was cooking loon for me, I'd specify Dutch Cleanser."

Not because I felt deeply indebted to him for a fine example of a rare decoy, but for sundry reasons of my own—we parted in agreement. The Loon, with the over long anchor line and a stone for ballast, came with me.

Due to geographic and coastal conditions, duck shooting on the upper coast of New England calls for pretty salty methods; particularly with reference to the gunning of sea ducks. To illustrate these methods, I will again resort to pictures, show diagrams of off-shore dory gunning together with typical Coot, Eider Duck and Old Squaw decoys from Monhegan Island, Maine, and Annisquam, Massachusetts.

For the most part the gunning of sea ducks is conducted on outlying ocean shoals, therefore in unsheltered water. It is essentially nautical and first of all one needs to be "a good sailor." The gunning craft is a sixteen foot "Cooting Dory" that rides safely in the heaviest off-shore swell. Procedure is cold and strenuous, but of great simplicity. In most instances a single trawl line, moored by a five-pronged graplin anchor, carries all the gear. The dory occupies a position about midway on the trawl with tollers to windward and leeward. The tollers ride one behind the other on the trawl, made fast by individual short lines. When birds are killed, the gunners cast off the dory, "pick up" and return to their buoy on the mooring line. It is cold hard work but has many followers.

For those unfamiliar with the practices of the upper coast

I show a picture of a "Cooting Dory" in action. A picture also permits me to show the painted Coot on the sides of the dory; a trick frequently adopted to camouflage and lower the visibility of a necessary but incongruous feature on the shoal. In making this illustration, I have followed a method established by a Monhegan Island skipper, well known for his simple painting of Island activities. (See Plate No. 72.)

The decoys of Monhegan receive special attention at the hands of their makers. There is no stinting of labor or material, no mail-order house construction, or taking some outsider's word for it. They are made locally and seemingly for all time. As a matter of fact, decoys similar to those shown in the accompanying plate are looked upon as heirlooms and passed down from father to son. If there are no sons, you marry the daughter.

Unlike the Nova Scotia tollers, these decoys have flat bottoms and heads are mortised into the body. Another feature of interest is the full and wide breast designed to give buoyancy where required to overcome the weight of the head and downward pull of the mooring line. The drawing of the Old Squaw in Plate No. 73 shows this feature clearly; an important item in the design of all decoys. The painting of Monhegan decoys is noticeable for its simplicity. There is no quibbling or minor shading, but plumage clearly and emphatically conveyed.

In some localities, the regulation tollers are amplified by the use of the so-called double or shadow decoys. This latter type may be described as duck profiles, cut from one inch plank and set up at each end of a short board or float. For convenience in stowing, these spreaders, or floats, are of graduated lengths so as to permit of nesting six pairs together. Spreaders vary in length from two feet six inches to about three feet. Fastening doubles to the mooring is accomplished by passing the main line through two fore and aft holes at the center of the float or spreader.

The gunners of Cape Ann have an ingenious method of

combining these shadow decoys with regular tollers. The trawl line is set in the form of the letter J, and maintained in position by a graplin at each extremity of the figure. About twelve solid decoys occupy the upper or standing part of the J, an equal number of double decoys the curved or lower end. Reference to the diagram on Plate No. 76 will show that shadows in this arrangement become visible in full profile from different points of the compass. Both blocks and shadows are attached at about ten foot intervals, permitting passage of the dory when retrieving birds. In this formation, the dory occupies a separate mooring, located in the space enclosed by the J.

The trawl line principle in gunning Sea Ducks is very much of a tradition. In various forms it may be found on northern coastal waters from Long Island Sound to Nova Scotia. The decoys employed have great variation in detail but are uniformly rugged and seaworthy. The old Coot shown in Plate No. 41 was made on Cape Ann by a Captain Gilbert Davis, back in 1870. Details of its use in connection with shadow decoys were furnished by its present owner, Captain John E. Stanwood, of Annisquam, Mass.

Another example of Yankee ingenuity appears in the huge Canada Goose decoys employed by "Stand Shooters" of eastern Massachusetts. In this purely New England practice, two sets of decoys are used—teams of live geese operated from the stand, and "slat geese" anchored far out on the pond or bay. In these modern times teams of live decoys number from 50 to 100 birds and constitute the principal feature of the system. The slat decoys act as outposts, remaining permanently at anchor from one end of the season to the other. Their purpose is to attract birds passing at a greater distance. To accomplish this, slat decoys are greatly oversize, ranging from three to four feet long and built to ride very high on the water.

The system operates by relays. The wild visitors, attracted to the pond by long-distance decoys, are enticed shoreward by live decoys operated from the stand, finally to be lured within gunshot by live geese flown from pens specially constructed for the purpose. It is a purely local method and confined to the lakes and ponds which are very numerous in this part of the State, particularly that region lying south-east of Boston. The subject, in all its many and historical angles is treated fully in a recent work by that able sporting historian—John C. Phillips.*

But the outpost decoys are also deserving of record. As shown by the accompanying photograph, their construction is both ingenious and practical. Instead of being made from solid timber, the hull or body is planked up on frames like a boat. At one time it was customary to cover the hull thus formed with canvas, but all such over-sized decoys are now made with slat siding only. Construction seldom varies. The planking, one-quarter inch thick, is applied to three forms or "frames" located respectively at the breast, amidships, and stern. The after form is in the nature of a transom with planks projecting to form the overhanging tail. The bottom, save for a single board about four inches wide, is left open. This board extends beyond the body six or eight inches at each end to provide for nailing to the mooring frame.

Slat decoys of this type are not anchored individually, but in groups of three, one at each apex of a triangular frame. The triangles are made of boards or cedar poles, eight to ten feet long on the sides, six to eight feet on the base. From four to eight of these frames are used, making a total of twelve to twenty-four decoys for a set. In position on open water, a fleet of decoys like these "loom" like battleships.

The slat decoy shown in Plate No. 77 is a typical example. The body dimensions are 3 feet 6 inches long, 13 inches wide, and 10 inches high. The head stands a full 13 inches above the breast. Its comparative visibility is indicated by the normal

*John C. Phillips, "Shooting Stands of Eastern Massachusetts." Privately printed at Cambridge, Mass., 1929.
Dr. Phillips estimates between 5,000 and 6,000 live Canada Geese in use as goose decoys in this State in 1929.

size Old Squaw decoy shown alongside. It is the work of Joseph W. Lincoln, a contemporary decoy maker of Accord, Mass. On a visit to Mr. Lincoln in 1931, I was informed that the older, canvas covered type was locally called "Butcher Carts" or barrel geese.

Curiously enough, I first became acquainted with Canvas Geese in Virginia, but they were a long way from home, having come originally from a small village on the shore of eastern Massachusetts. Here, although abandoned in connection with barrel decoys, slat construction covered with canvas for geese of normal size is very much in favor. The custom still clings to New England, seemingly a left-over from the tradition and proclivities of ship-building. At first glance this built-up type of body seems difficult and expensive to make but systematic procedure proves otherwise. No labor or material is wasted and the result is a decoy of high visibility, light weight and great practicability.

Unlike the outer decoys of stand shooting, these decoys are designed to ride at individual anchors. They are provided with a watertight bottom and the planking covered with heavy duck and painted, exactly as in the construction of a canvas canoe. To demonstrate how this is accomplished, I show a typical goose body without the final covering, in Plate No. 78.

As in boat building, it is necessary to predetermine all forms to receive future planking. If this preliminary model or layout work is accurately done, fair lines and success are assured. In this type the body frames are secured to a bottom board of $\frac{7}{8}$ inch white pine or cedar. The forward frame, in the form of a full rounded breast, is cut from a solid block and rebated to receive the ends of the planking. The after frame carries a solid overhang member to give the required tail. The midship frame is cut from $\frac{5}{8}$ inch plank.

The planking employed is of bass-wood, slightly less than $\frac{1}{8}$ inch thick and shaped as required by the spacing on the frames. It is sprung to shape and copper fastened. The canvas is applied in one piece, fitted at the front, lapped and finished at the breast by a single sewn seam. In securing this coat-like form, the material is lapped about ½ inch on the under-side of the bottom and fastened with closely spaced copper tacks. A good workman obtains a neat job without wrinkles or other imperfections. The head is secured to the body by a ½ inch dowel, reinforced by a single screw in forward part of the head base.

The "Bag Decoy" is another eastern coast invention, said to have originated on the marshes of Cape Cod and used principally in the gunning of Black Duck. Bag decoys are extremely simple to make and when used in company with block decoys, very effective. They are literally bags—made of unbleached cotton or light weight duck, and stuffed with dry grass or granulated cork. The bags are not cylindrical but something like a wide-mouthed jug, about 20 inches long and painted a dull black. After filling, the open end is tied tightly with tarred line. About three inches of the material is left projecting beyond the tie to convey the impression of a head. The tying cord is left long for attachment to the trawl or mooring line. These decoys are very light and convenient to carry. Five or six of them on a line make a most effective showing.

One accustomed to standard decoys is constantly impressed by this peculiar ingenuity of the New England gunner. I, for one, find it a fascinating and instructive subject. In support of this, I once saw a Cape Cod Sheldrake with a crest made of horse hair. It had come to rest in the window of an antique shop in the village of Chatham. The decoy was very old and battered. The paint had all but disappeared and the neck was split. At a guess, I should say that the decoy was 50 years old. It was a drake, and a very gay old bird, for the horsehair crest was still intact, leaded into a saw-cut at the top of the broken head.

To conclude remarks on decoy makers of the Upper Coast, I will again refer to Stratford, Connecticut. The old-time

PLATE 87
MALE WHISTLER SCOOTER DECOY *by Wilbur R. Corwin*
Bellport, L. I., about 1886

PLATE 88
FEMALE WHISTLER SCOOTER DECOY *by Wilbur R. Corwin*
Bellport, L. I., about 1886

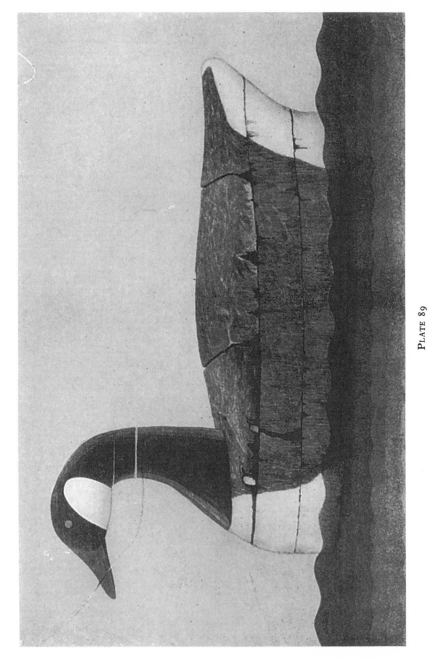

PLATE 89

CORK CANADA GOOSE *by Captain John Whittaker*

Great South Bay, L. I., 1880

decoys of this locality were very fine. Who established the original standards I am not prepared to say, but whoever did so had a firm hand. The Blue-bill shown in Plate No. 80 for example, is nearly 60 years old and still treasured as a fine decoy. From the original maker it passed into the hands of a local gunner named "Cappie Wicks;" years later descended to the son, "Young Cappie." Through the courtesy of the son, I painted this picture and a long time afterwards acquired the old Blue-bill for my collection. This decoy is one of a group awarded a "Gold Medal" at the Philadelphia Centennial Exposition in 1876. The maker was Benjamin Holmes of Stratford.

In my collection are other decoys from this locality, by other men but of equally fine workmanship and design. Principal among these is the Black Duck by a man named Laing shown in Plate No. 47. It is also of interest to know that the high standards established by Ben Holmes and his contemporaries still persist. A few years ago another Stratford maker received similar recognition—this time a "Silver Cup" carrying the following inscription:

AWARDED
By
ANTI DUSKERS
TO
CHARLES E. WHEELER

Champion Amateur
DECOY MAKER
of
Suffolk County, N. Y.
1923

This cup was presented at Bellport, Long Island, by a group of sportsmen who organized the first decoy show ever held in America. Decoys were assembled from many sections of the country and the award made for the best decoy of the show. The drake Mallard shown in Plate No. 34 is one of the winning pair, made by Charles E. Wheeler of Stratford, Conn. Mr. Wheeler's skill as decoy maker and plumage painter is well known, and here at the end of observations on New England, I show examples of his work.

The decoys selected for illustration are part of a large group made for an exhibition which took place during the Fall of 1931. The show, under the auspices of The Abercrombie & Fitch Company, was held in the log cabin penthouse on the roof of their New York store. The idea was to have a joint display of old and new decoys. "Shang" Wheeler and myself were the sole contributors. My own exhibit consisted of a large group of old and historical decoys, 116 in all; Mr. Wheeler's 21 pairs of new decoys, including geese and swan. Accompanying these were Wheeler's prize winners of other exhibitions and a group of "Rough and Ready" cork decoys.

The exhibition was of great interest to sportsmen and others. For the first time in the history of wild fowling, the full range of American decoys were assembled for comparison. No one can represent the decoys of modern times like Mr. Wheeler. Decoy making with him is a continuance of a fine community tradition. It seems fitting, therefore, to illustrate his decoys, in company with earlier New England workmanship.

REGIONAL DECOYS

LONG ISLAND

... "It's way across the bay, Mister
And only a lean-to shanty;
Not even painted except the door—
Nothing around but salt meadow
And gulls and Black Duck in the fall.
It takes a boat to get there
And it's full of old decoys.
You couldn't use it Mister and anyway—
The place is not for sale."*

Along the middle and lower Atlantic Coast, protected by outer barriers of sand dunes, lie a series of narrow land-locked bays. The waters are shoal and brackish. At irregular intervals, inlets from the ocean maintain a slight rise and fall of tide. The mainland shores are low, vignetted with salt meadows and marshes. Since time immemorial these waters have been the winter feeding grounds of millions of migratory waterfowl.

The most northerly of these reaches occur in the vicinity of New York, extending along the southerly side of Long Island, the Great South Bay, Moriches Bay and Shinnecock Bay. They cover a distance of approximately 60 miles and are connected by narrow grass-grown channels.

On these waters many species of wild ducks and great numbers of wild geese, spend the winter. The low lying shores of the mainland and sandy beaches on the ocean side serve also as feeding grounds for myriads of migratory shore birds. One should, however, describe this region in terms of the past. Due to the advance of civilization, the number of wild visitors is now greatly reduced. At one time, however, these waters and shores were the habitat of professional fowlers and resort of sportsmen. Before the day of Federal restrictions, gunning was continuous from the arrival of birds in the fall to their de-

*Queen Anne's *Record,* "No Sale."

parture in the spring. It was Long Island that supplied the
New York game markets for over a century. In the history of
American duck shooting, therefore, it occupies a position of
importance. In printed records it also appears as the cradle
of our American system.

Here in 'longshore villages were baymen who made their
living by fishing and fowling. Decoys were the commonplace
tools of their homely trade. Every community had its stool
makers. Decoys were roughly made but sturdy and above everything effective, a lowly but necessary implement of tide-water
activity. But what Long Island decoys lacked in quality was
made up in effectiveness and variety. Being decoy minded, it
is not strange that the use of decoys was carried to extremes—
some of them worthy of special description.

While Long Island favored decoys of the solid type, the
hollow decoy came into use for winter gunning in the so-called
"ice scooter," a ducking boat used only on these waters. Described briefly, the Great South Bay scooter is similar to a
sneak-box but with flatter bottom and higher domed deck to
conceal the gunner. The hull is equipped with metal-shod run-
ners, in other words designed to travel on water or ice, or as
frequently happens—both. The equipment consists of a sprit
sail, oars and a specially shod shoving pole. Boat, spars, etc.,
are painted white and the gunner wears white outer clothing.

The operation of these boats is extremely hazardous and
undertaken only by baymen of long experience. When the bay
is frozen over or the waters choked with floating ice, they are
very effective in the pursuit of birds which congregate in the
small stretches of open water. The element of danger, however, is great and equipment must be of the least possible dead
weight. For this reason, the decoys carried on board are somewhat undersized and frequently of hollow construction.

The pair of Whistlers shown in Plates Nos. 87 and 88 are
typical examples of scooter decoys. They were made at Bellport, Long Island, in the year 1875 by Captain Wilbur R.

PLATE 90
SWIMMING SHELDRAKE
Great South Bay, L. I.

PLATE 91
SHELDRAKE IN SPRING PLUMAGE *by Frank Kellum*
Babylon, L. I., 1890

OLD STICK-UP GULL   PLATE 92   SHELDRAKE

From Martha's Vineyard, Mass.

PLATE 93

STICK-UP GULL *by Frank Kellum*

Babylon, L. I., 1890

Corwin. The bodies are of white cedar, hollow, and weigh with ballast 18 ounces each. The bottoms are flat to permit of setting out on the ice bordering open water.

But Long Islanders have always favored decoys of solid construction, and this explains, perhaps, the adoption of natural cork as a material for decoys of minimum weight. The use of cork is one of the few innovations accepted by this sophisticated region. It was first confined to crude Black Duck decoys, little more than floats equipped with heads. Originally material came from old life preservers salvaged along the outer beaches. If the pieces of cork were too small, two or three sections were used, pegged to a shaped bottom board of pine. Beginning with Black Duck, the use of cork was soon extended to the making of geese, later to other species.

One of the oldest cork decoys to come to my attention is the Shinnecock Black Duck illustrated in Plate No. 44. I have no data as to age or maker. It was a derelict picked up on the ocean beach of Shinnecock many years ago. It was old then, but one of the first full-bodied cork decoys I had ever seen. The hull consists of a white cedar core or inner form, veneered with cork about one inch thick. The accompanying diagram shows details of construction.

The oldest cork decoy to my knowledge with a recorded date is the grand old "Whittaker Goose" shown in Plate No. 89. It was made by Captain John Whittaker of Amityville in 1898, one of a set of twelve geese decoys still in the possession of the family and reproduced through the courtesy of Mr. John Whittaker of New York.

Progress in the making of cork decoys is indicated by the Thomas Gelston Black Duck shown in Plate No. 43, made at Quogue, L. I., about 1897. Even more modern is the work of Mr. Charles E. Wheeler as shown by the Black Duck and Coot decoys of Plate No. 83. These modern decoys represent what is perhaps the final stage of development in construction of cork decoys.

Discussion of Long Island methods of decoy making should also include the custom of cutting decoy heads from green pine knots. It was applied principally in making Brant and Sheldrake heads but included also the long necked heads of Canada Geese. It originated no doubt in a desire to overcome the constant splitting of heads made in the customary manner. In heads made from knots, all cross grain is eliminated, making them practically indestructible. The use of natural shapes also gave a desirable variety of poses.

The original pine-knot heads were apparently made for Brant decoys, an industry having a queer but little known angle. In the old days they were made neither by gunner nor decoy maker, but by isolated dwellers in the scrub pine regions north of the old Merrick Road. Every fall these inland head makers would drive down to the landings and sell their product. I am told by old gunners that many years ago these men would appear with burlap bags filled with heads that sold at 5 cents apiece, then 9 cents, finally mounting toward the end to 25 cents. Apparently it was a sort of a leisure hour pursuit. When spring shooting was prohibited in 1913, production ceased.

In making these heads, freshly cut green timber was used, small "scrub pine" trees averaging about 4 inches in diameter. The felled trees were first cut in short lengths, each section having one branch suitable to form the bill. After roughly trimming with a hatchet, the blocks were boiled to eliminate pitch and soften the wood. The boiling process also did away with the tendency of freshly cut timber to check in process of drying. When dried out, knots treated in this manner were easily roughed out by a hatchet and finished with a knife in the usual fashion.

To illustrate the feature of variety of pose obtained by the use of pine knots, I show three old decoys from the vicinity of Babylon. The swimming Sheldrake in Plate No. 90 is a typical example of the older type. It was presented to the author by Mr. Duncan Arnold of West Islip. During the scarcity of decoys which occurred in the season following the World War, it had been acquired with a miscellaneous group of old decoys to fill the ranks of a depleted battery rig. Mr. Arnold could give me no history. From appearance, however, one can assume that it was a product of the 'eighties.

The male Sheldrake in full plumage shown in Plate No. 91 is of much later date, probably about 1900. It came into my possession through Captain Andrew Sammis of Babylon, who for many years operated the gunning rig of Colonel A. V. Post of New York. To the best of Captain Andrew's recollection it was made by "one of the Haff family" of Islip, L. I.

Long Island customs also went so far as to include Sea Gull lures, some of them fine examples of the decoy maker's art. These decoys were of two types, floating and stick-up. They were employed principally in the old Brant rigs operated on the westerly and brackish waters of the Great South Bay. A Gull stool was considered a good omen. Stuck up on a neighboring sand bar, or anchored to one side of the main rig, the presence of a Gull was supposed to verify the illusion that all was well. I cannot vouch for this assumption. To me, Gull decoys represent a gesture of superstition, a gunner's lucky piece rather than a lure. To record the custom, however, I illustrate three examples of Gull decoys. As previously noted, the floating Gull shown in Plate No. 37 was employed on the waters off Amityville. Although without actual records it dates back to the early years of Long Island market gunning. As far as can be learned it was made during the 'seventies.

While very primitive, and of undoubted antiquity, the stick-up Gull shown in Plate No. 92 lacks data as to history. In this respect it is an unusual item of my collection, as all details as to locality, date and maker are unknown. In collecting decoys one can usually find one or more items of history, at least the waters on which the decoys were used. But here, nothing. It came into my possession through a New York art dealer, acquired as an example of primitive American Sculpture. It is merely a grand old decoy, made by a man in a hurry perhaps, but who knew his trade.

The third Gull shown in Plate No. 93 is reproduced through the courtesy of Mr. Frederick Becker of Babylon. It came from one of the old professional rigs of this locality, the work of a local decoy maker by the name of Frank Kellum. Kellum was a well known and picturesque figure of the 'nineties, and apparently very talented. So much so, that a group of New York sportsmen of the Old Wy-wy-an-da Club became interested and made it possible for him to go to New York to study art. Many stories are told of this episode, but it appears that the idea didn't work out. Kellum had always followed the water and soon came back to it. What he knew of guns and boats, decoys and the Great South Bay, was enough for any man. The art of schools meant nothing at all to him.

On the Great South Bay Gull decoys were also employed by so-called "feather hunters," gunners who hunted to trim hats of ladies of the day. In recent years ladies shoot ducks, but not those of the 'nineties. That was a day when fine feathers made fine birds, not sportswomen. But the ladies have never accepted decoys, satisfied no doubt as to the effectiveness of personal charms.

Before leaving decoys of Long Island shores, there is one more item to be recorded—the so-called high-boy or Blue Heron decoys shown in the accompanying plate. Here and there along the bay, old lures for the "sweet-fleshed" Heron may still be found. These unusual decoys are supposed to have originated from emergency devices, made on the spot from driftwood. I illustrate the procedure in Plate No. 94. The body is half a barrel head, the neck a hoop, the whole supported by a split stave. Sometimes the barrel head was reversed, having the circular edge down to permit of draping the upper side with seaweed in semblance of plumage. Standing motionless in a likely spot the illusion of a Blue Heron is little short of perfection.

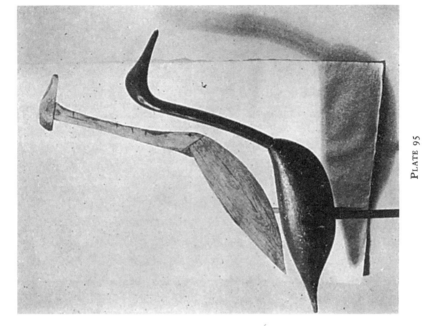

PLATE 95

PRIMITIVE BLUE HERON, JERSEY SHORE (above)

BLUE HERON (below)

Jones Beach, L. I.

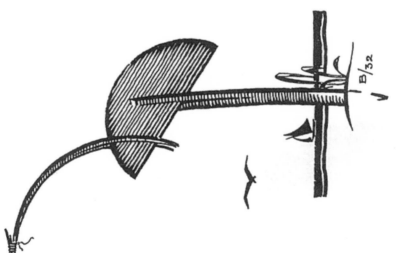

B/32

PLATE 94

DRIFTWOOD HERON

PLATE 96
FEMALE SHELDRAKE *by Capt. Cooper Predmore*
Barnegat Village, N. J., about 1880

PLATE 97
BRANT
Barnegat Bay, 1895

REGIONAL DECOYS

Permanent Heron decoys are rather rare but not impossible to find. The one picture in the background of Plate No. 95 shows a primitive type of much interest. It came originally from the Jersey Coast, down Barnegat way and is reproduced here through the courtesy of its present owner, Mr. J. J. Halle of New York. The decoy in the foreground is more sophisticated. The long neck and head is worked from a natural crook, and being tenoned into the body is demountable. The color is bluish gray. This grand old Heron came from the vicinity of Jones Beach, now a State park and during the summer months, the resort of thousands of pleasure seekers. My Blue Heron is a survivor of other days. Times have changed. Gulls and Herons are protected by kindly laws. The one wheels unhunted in the sky; the other, in strange immobility, goes his solitary way, unharmed.

BARNEGAT

A few miles south of New York on the Jersey Coast lies Barnegat Bay, another concentration point for migratory waterfowl, another resort of native and visiting fowlers. Barnegat extends from Bay Head to Atlantic City, a distance of approximately fifty miles. Like its neighbor on the north, it is protected by an outer barrier of sand dunes and its shoal and brackish water is maintained by inlets from the ocean. It is equally accessible from New York and Philadelphia, but during the winter months seems very remote, even lonelier than the Great South Bay. But for generations of duck shooters there has been romance even in the name of "Barnegat."

Due no doubt to its peculiar isolation, Barnegat is a region of fixed standards and fashions, particularly with respect to boat building and decoy making. Both of these activities are very strongly marked. In a previous chapter I have described the Jersey methods of decoy construction and conditions which produced them. Here I shall show a few specific examples to indicate their principal characteristics. In doing so I will call attention to the strong family resemblance which occurs in decoys of the Jersey shore.

While all decoys made by hand carry the personal touch of the maker, Barnegat has a wider and regional quality that is unmistakable. I found one once on the shore of Connecticut, more definitely in the boat house of my friend, "Shang" Wheeler at Milford. It was after the gunning season and the rig of several hundred decoys were stored in a loft, some in barrels, others piled in the gable end. Most of them were of local make but one very obviously had a foreign source. In taking it out of a barrel I remarked: "Here is a lady a long way from home." Mr. Wheeler, out of his wide experience, identified it instantly by the single word "Barnegat."

To show these regional characteristics several decoys are illustrated. Plate No. 15 pictures a Jersey dugout made about 1880 and of typical 'longshore origin. The maker, Captain Cooper Predmore of Barnegat Village, was for many years master of a ship in the coastal lumber trade. In later life he retired to the Coast Guard Service, in charge of the Love Ladies Station, at that time located just south of the present Barnegat Light. It was at this period that the pictured decoys were made—more than 50 years ago.

So fixed are the standards of this region that the Shang Wheeler decoy might well have been a wayward sister. The drake Sheldrake of Plate No. 96 is another Predmore decoy from the same rig. Both decoys were loaned for reproduction by Mr. Grove Conrad, grandson of the maker and still resident of Barnegat.

Color Plate C gives a Canada Goose stool of the 'nineties; and Plate No. 97 a typical Brant of about the same period. Both are very fine decoys and both were taken from rigs of professional gunners. Like all collectors, I take great pleasure in acquiring specimens. I carried that Goose back to New York, wrapped in a second-hand sheet of brown paper, too small to cover or disguise the Goose. Fellow travelers were amused but

PLATE 98
BARNEGAT DECOYS
BROADBILL AND BLACK DUCK   OLD REDHEAD
by Henry Kilpatrick   *Maker Unknown*

Barnegat Bay

PLATE 99
DECOY HEAD IN BRONZE *by the Author*
From an old Jersey decoy

PLATE 100
MALE CANVAS-BACK *by Robert F. McGaw*
Havre de Grace, Md., 1929

PLATE 101
FEMALE CANVAS-BACK *by Robert F. McGaw*
Havre de Grace, Md., 1929

any possible embarrassment was overcome by the pleasure of possession.

Plate No. 98 shows three decoys, Black Duck, Blue-bill and Redhead. The Redhead at the lower left comes from Tuckerton but is not of local make. It was picked up, adrift on the bay, made, no doubt, farther south. The Black Duck, top, and the Blue-bill, are the work of Henry Kilpatrick, boat builder, fisherman and decoy maker of Barnegat Village. These last decoys may be classed as modern work. If I remember correctly they were made in 1920–21 entirely by hand in the original Jersey fashion and described under the heading of hollow decoys.

I have said in passing that Barnegat decoys are all of a similar pattern, but that statement is not quite correct. Decoys from the lower end of the bay have another look, more variation and a rather queer turn. By some of the more traditional makers, these exceptions are subject to smiling criticism, but to me they are of great interest. Those found along the upper bay are mostly derelict decoys picked up after southerly storms. I have never visited below Tuckerton but have several examples of the decoys. They were made supposedly by men of the barrens further south.

One of these decoys is shown in Plate No. 32, a Black Duck, very old with a body designed to receive the skin of a bird in lieu of painted plumage. The head is rough but striking.

In Plate No. 99 I show a decoy head cast in bronze. I whittled it myself but used as a model an old decoy from the lower Jersey Coast. The body of this decoy was little more than a float to receive a skin but the head was very fine. My jack-knife copy of this head reproduced in bronze was sold by art galleries over a period of several years and in considerable numbers. I have always considered the unknown original maker a real artist. Even though he lived and worked, unknown on the Jersey barrens, his Black Duck head has been perpetuated. The feather of accomplishment does not belong to me. I merely whittled what he conceived. After a fashion, however, it vindicates my interest in the art of decoy making. The decoy itself is now a highly prized item of my collection. After my coveting it for several years, the former owner, Mr. J. H. Phillips of Babylon, gave it to me for my records of Barnegat Bay.

Barnegat, like other coastal gunning grounds, has changed greatly in recent years. In the spring of the year when birds congregate before leaving for the North, one may gain some idea of its former glory as a winter feeding ground. But gunning here has fallen in line with times, conditions and laws. Due to the past, however, it is a field of great interest to the collector of wild fowl history and wild fowl decoys.

THE CHESAPEAKE

"On summer evenings, when the log canoe
   Rides black against the Chesapeake moon,
   And the wind is southerly,
   And the water sounds like children sleeping;
With Rose laughing in the shanty boat
And niggers talking soft and singing low—
It's good enough and bad enough for me."*

Chesapeake Bay and Canvas-back are inseparable. Canvasback shooting on the Susquehanna Flats is a classic of American wild fowling. There is no other region quite like it. In the shoal waters of these great "flats," the abundant growth of wild celery makes of it the principal resort of Canvas-back and Redhead on the Atlantic Coast. Birds killed on these feeding grounds are rated higher than any other waterfowl in the world. The gunning area at the head of the Chesapeake includes similar flats caused by other important tributaries which empty their waters into the main estuary, but those of Susquehanna are the most famous. The Village of Havre de Grace at the mouth of the river has been for many years the headquarters of pro-

*Queen Anne's *Record*.

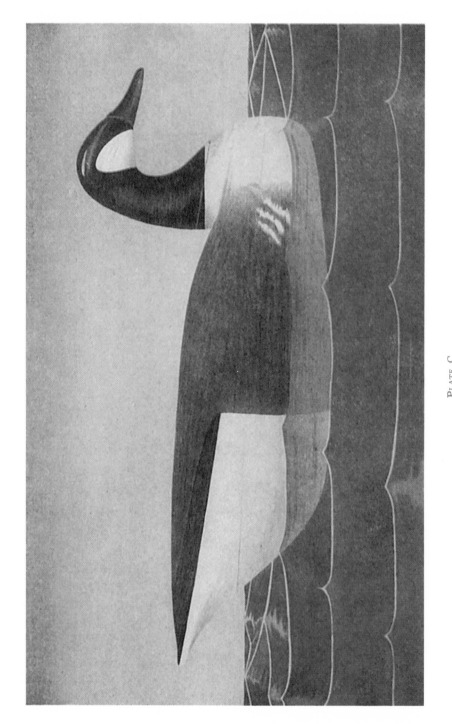

Plate C

CANADA GOOSE, BARNEGAT BAY, 1890

fessional gunners and sportsmen. Even in these days of change and restrictions, Havre de Grace remains the centre of activity.

During the scarcity of decoys which occurred after the World War, this section was unaffected. The number of decoys on hand at the termination of market gunning in 1918 was enormous. The retirement of professional battery rigs at this time meant more than enough for Canvas-back shooting in the restricted form of sport. To gain some idea of the situation, it will be remembered that each battery employed hundreds of stool ducks. To reproduce the impression of the great rafts of Canvas-back which assemble on the flats, each rig required from 250 to 500 units. It was not unusual for one professional to have a thousand decoys in his equipment, all made locally and by hand. The mere handling them on the bay was a highly specialized feature of the business.

My visits to Havre de Grace have been of great interest. It is more than a harbor of Grace, it is a port of wild-fowling history, old decoys and decoy makers. One expects to find things here and is never disappointed. Decoys bob up everywhere, even in off seasons, one finds them in boat-houses, lofts, backyard shanties and piled along the waterfront; literally thousands of them, and for the most part Canvas-back.

Nearly all of these decoys have strong family or regional characteristics. They are of solid construction, generally cut from white pine blocks 4×6×12 inches. A slightly larger standard runs 4×7×13 inches. Bottoms have a dead rise section with lead or iron ballast placed well aft. The anchor fastening consists of a galvanized iron ring and staple; anchor lines are about 12 feet long. Average weight of decoys, including ballast, runs to three pounds. The painting is very simple and seldom varies. Each rig includes only from 12 to 15 per cent females. Too many females darken the impression and cut down visibility. The large proportion of male plumage keeps the set lighter in color.

The Chesapeake battery decoy is a very superior article.

The area covered by the set is too great to watch or care for imperfect units. If stool become overturned or go adrift— that's just too bad. In course of time therefore, faults have been eliminated. In the frontispiece I show a typical Susquehanna Canvas-back made during the 'eighties. The maker's name is unknown to me but local legend insists that Grover Cleveland, most sporting of United States Presidents, killed many and prime Canvas-back over the rig to which it belonged. I have a pair of these Cleveland souvenirs and value them highly. After considerable search they were located by a friend living at Aiken, Maryland, and familiar with many historical features of the region. They were found at North East, a village on the North East River which empties into the Bay to the east of Havre de Grace. The present owner, Mr. A. J. Reynolds of North East, kindly loaned them for reproduction.

Another example of about the same period is the Canvas-back shown in Plate No. 11. This decoy is attributed to Captain Ben Dye, a well-known Havre de Grace maker of the 'eighties. Plates Nos. 100 to 102 show contemporary Canvas-back by Robert F. McGaw of Havre de Grace. These decoys indicate the modern tendencies of the region. The heads are appreciably higher than in the older decoys and new features appear in the body. The side lines, for instance, have much less sweep, and less material is cut away at breast and tail. By this procedure higher visibility is obtained, also greater stability by the longer fore and aft bearing.

The comparatively straight-sided body is now an accepted feature of battery decoys. In stowing on board the stool boat, anchor lines are wound around the body to prevent fouling and on the old decoys the turns of the lines had a tendency to slip off. The new type with straight and parallel sides, holds the lines securely, thus doing away with much inconvenience.

The Canvas-back decoys of this region show many and similar features of excellence arrived at through the process of evolution. Here one also finds queer offshoots of the main

PLATE 102

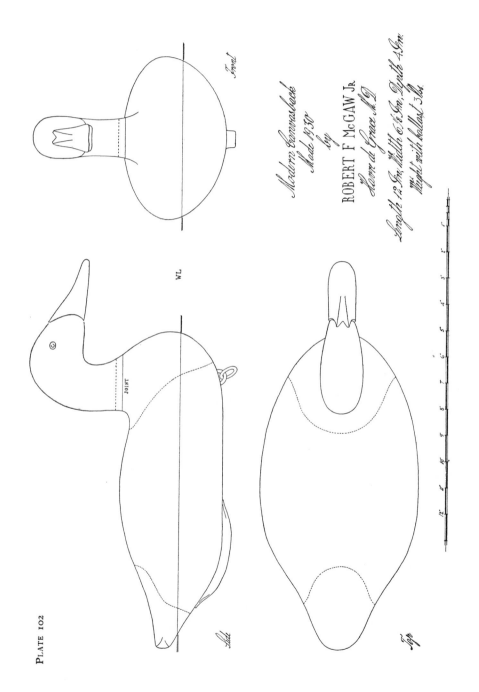

WL

Front

Joint

Side

Top

Modern Canvasback
Made 1930
by
ROBERT F McGAW Jr.
Havre de Grace M.D.

Length 12 In. Width 6⅛ In. Depth 4 In.
Weight with ballast 3 lbs.

PLATE 103
WILD PIGEONS *by Joseph Coudon*
Aiken, Md., about 1875

PLATE 104
WILD SWAN *by Samuel T. Barnes*
Havre de Grace, Md., about 1890

issue. The pair of Wild Pigeon decoys of Plate No. 103 is an example. As the Wild Pigeon is now extinct, these old carvings take on a special significance. As far as I know they are the only authentic "stool pigeon" in America.

These rare decoys came to light in the attic of a fine old house at the head of the Bay and are reproduced through the courtesy of their maker, Mr. Joseph Coudon, of Aiken, Maryland. In the role of native sportsman Mr. Coudon, the son of Henry Coudon, has participated in many branches of Chesapeake fowling. His experience goes back to the days of muzzle loading 8 gauge shot guns and the handmade decoys of a fastidious sporting family. And they were very fine decoys. His first toy, for example, was a handsome little Blue-bill made by his father. The Black-head, as he calls it, is over 70 years old now, battered, worn and marked by the teeth of puppy dogs. "It has never been overboard," the owner tells me—"just a plaything."

As the passenger pigeon was passing out of the American picture, Mr. Coudon and his elder brother made the pigeon of the illustration. As a matter of record, I quote a portion of his letter under date of February 4, 1930, with respect to the episode:

"This may be of personal interest to you. Today I found in the attic, a box containing about three dozen wooden birds that I and my brother made for decoys. They are more than half a century old and were made for decoys and used as such. Among them are represented black birds, larks, doves and wild pigeons. They all did service at the time they were made and a few succeeding seasons.

"There is a hole in the under part of the pigeons and doves. We planted the top of a small dead tree in a buckwheat or Hungarian grass patch to hold up the decoys. This was all arranged nicely by cutting the ends of the perpendicular branches to fit the holes. After arranging this, we would make a blind and wait for the birds to come. . . . If you do not want to see some of these birds, notify me in time to stop shipment."

In this way one acquires items of historical interest. It is needless to say that the shipment was not stopped, and Wild Pigeon came into the record of American decoys.

In his later years Mr. Coudon has turned to the serenity of conservation. He no longer shoots or makes decoys, but carries on tradition in the carving and painting of game birds and game panels. His interest has wide scope and his work carries distinction, but his favorite subject is Canvas-back, the treasure and legacy of his locality.

In the Susquehanna region, where decoy making has flourished uninterrupted for over a hundred years one will find these unusual examples of the Maryland gunner's art. The Wild Swan shown in Plate No. 104 is one of them. It was made some 40 years ago by the late Samuel T. Barnes, a well known gunner and decoy maker of Havre de Grace. For many years after retirement it ornamented the side yard of an old white house in Washington Street. It stood in front of a grape arbor, faded white and inconspicuous, at the same time very grand. And it belonged there, a retired aristocrat of the Bay. But after all, I am a collector and Swan decoys are the rarest of all. It seemed to me that day that I had discovered, to quote Frank Forester: "The King of waterfowl—the superb and incomparable Wild Swan."

The owner, Mr. Bennett Keen, was a retired gunner, sportsman and a generous trader. The deal took a little time, but a thing like that takes time; discussion of New York, decoys in general and in particular, to say nothing of the subject of the Susquehanna Flats. But the trade was satisfactory to both sides. I left the Swan, however, behind me. In spite of the pleasure of acquisition, here was a find too big and too grand to carry away. The day following, my friend Bob McGaw made a crate, and it travelled to New York by express. It has since appeared in several exhibitions and been frequently illustrated. At the present time it occupies a place of honor on

PLATE 105
BLUE-WING TEAL *by Charles T. Wilson*
Havre de Grace, Md., about 1900

PLATE 106
MALLARD DRAKE *by John Blair*
Delaware Bay, 1866

PLATE 107
MALLARD DUCK *by John Blair*
Delaware Bay, 1866

PLATE 108
OLD PINTAIL
Elkton, Md.

the top of a rosewood cabinet. Even here, in rigid chocks, it floats majestically.

Swan decoys are among the rarest on the coast, found only along the shores of the Chesapeake, Back Bay, Virginia, and Currituck Sound. Swan shooting has never been classed as a sport or business, most of those killed being the result of chance encounters by gunners in pursuit of other birds. Swan, however, are subject to attraction by decoys, particularly the tender fleshed young birds (cygnets). And here and there the rigs of professional gunners included a few Swan decoys. When Swan shooting was prohibited in 1913, many of these men knocked off the long heads and converted their swan into geese. Those that remain are few and far between.

Another rarity among the host of American stool ducks is the Blue- and Green-winged Teal.

Handmade Teal decoys are curiously hard to find. Except for those produced by western factories, very few were ever made. This may be due to the fact that Teal, both Blue- and Green-winged, will dart to other species, or perhaps because they slip along too fast to warrant the making of lures. Whatever the reason, Teal decoys on the Atlantic coast are very rare.

But still a few were made and used. On Plate No. 33 I show the stick-up Teal from Long Island and on Plate No. 105 a pair of floating Blue-wings from Maryland. Curiously they are not the work of a regular decoy maker, but made by the late Professor Charles T. Wilson of Havre de Grace. I look upon them as rare and very fine decoys. They are thirty, perhaps forty years old.

When discovered they occupied a shelf in a small store room at the rear of Bob McGaw's paint shop in Havre de Grace. I shall always think I was enticed there to see if I would spot them, surrounded by the miscellaneous gear of a waterman's belongings. Of course I saw them; what collector wouldn't. "Take 'em along," said Bob, and that was that. The school teacher Teal were thus added to the collection.

But some very outstanding decoys were made by men other than established decoy makers, principally sportsmen. The pair of Mallards shown in Plates Nos. 106 and 107 are examples. These very fine Mallards are the work of the late Mr. John Blair of Philadelphia and Elkton, Maryland. The set to which they belong was made in the year 1866 for use on the marshes of the Delaware. Of hollow construction, they are sort of a cross between Barnegat and the Chesapeake. The pair illustrated were loaned for reproduction by Mr. John Blair, Jr. of New York.

In discussing the work of his father, Mr. Blair explained the fine condition of the original painting. After nearly seventy years it was still perfect. It appears while the decoys were made by his father, the painting was done by a Philadelphia portrait painter of considerable note. The result was so fine that Blair, Sr., had individual canvas bags made to protect them. To this day, when not in use each member of the rig is stored in a bag.

Mr. Blair later presented me with the Pintail Drake diagrammed on Plate No. 50 and photographed on Plate No. 6. This was also made by his father, similar in construction and painted by the artist. Old Sprig decoys are rare but the Blair family certainly had them. On a visit to the old farm below Elkton on the estuary of the Elk River, another tributary of the Susquehanna Flats, I found the ancient Sprig shown in Plate No. 108. Mr. Walter, who occupies the farm, could tell me very little about its history. It appears that the oldest decoys on the farm were a legacy from an old man named Maxwell, a so-called "tenant gunner" who for many years occupied a shanty on the shore below the house. The old Pintail had belonged to him. I found it in the loft of the farm work shop, made fast to a long triangular frame in company with other but commonplace decoys. Someone at sometime had painted it black all over. When the black was removed all evidence of the original painting disappeared. On one side only there were traces of a wing splash.

The "wing-duck" Canvas-back shown on Plate No. 12 is another courtesy of Walter Blair. This decoy dates back to a very early period of Chesapeake history when flat bodied wooden decoys were spiked to the decks of batteries; a custom long since abandoned in favor of heavy decoys of cast iron. When I found it, someone had added a roughly shaped piece on the bottom to build up the body to a normal thickness.

The visit to the Blair farm produced one other and interesting souvenir, the small but unusually good Blue-bill shown in Plate No. 109. The painting is excellent, very similar to the pattern employed by the Great South Bay gunners for the drake "Broadbill." For ballast, however, it carries the old fashioned iron keel of Chesapeake Canvas-back.

Details as to age or makers of these relics were not available, but even in this locality of decoy making, they are outstanding examples of old time work. They are also reminders of that winter visit to a water-side farm that included among its traditions a "tenant gunner."

The Swan shown in Plate No. 110 is another example of farm decoy. It came to light in the granary loft of Mr. Owen B. Winters' farm on the Eastern shore of Maryland below Kent Island. It was a grand place, that loft, a forgotten store house of farmer gunners of an older order. Most of the decoys were no longer used, thrown one side like other broken down equipment. They consisted mostly of Canvas-back and so-called "Wiffler" (Whistler), many of them headless and otherwise broken. Some were good, or had been, others terrible, the work perhaps of unskilled farmer boys. Among these derelicts, the great old Swan stood out, like a lighthouse in a fog.

Mr. Ralph Whaley, former owner of the farm, could tell me little—"one of the old decoys on the farm," nothing more. It had been there as long as he could remember, unused and forgotten since the law against the killing of Swan some twenty years before. In his opinion, however, it was about 40 years old, a fine example of decoy making during the 'nineties. With the broken head restored, it represents in royal fashion the singular and marine-like quality which occurs in the best of American decoys.

On Plate No. 61, showing "weights and anchors," is another decoy from the Winters farm, the one at the bottom of the picture. There were many interesting decoys in this old loft and subsequently a number of them were used for decorative purposes in the living room of the main house on the point. But this one came to New York. It is intended no doubt to serve the dual purpose of Blue-bill and Whistler. The wedge-shaped body carries a really fine head in excellent pose but the painting is very unusual. Blue-bill, Whistler—male and female patterns are mixed. One can call it one or the other or both. The body is a sooty black and faded white, the head of neutral brown, but the result is simple and effective. It also carries the "mule shoe keel" of this particular region, and taken altogether is a very interesting specimen.

Several years before securing this decoy, I came across this same idea of dual plumage, this time illustrated in a Blue-bill painted in such a fashion as to serve both male and female purposes. This example came from lower down the Chesapeake and into my possession in a rather curious way.

On two or three occasions, vague stories had reached me about an old Virginia gunner, who was forever combing the beaches to find materials from which to make decoys for which he was famous. According to the legend, the bodies of his decoys were made principally from old spars which came ashore on the beach. For heads he employed odds and ends of drift wood as suited his fancy, many of them being made from queer shaped knots or sections of twisted roots. One of my informants, Captain Andrew Sammis, had encountered him on a gunning trip to Virginia many years ago. My interest in decoys and decoy making jogged his memory—the surname was Cobb.

The next incident took a more definite form. Another Captain, Captain Paul Curtis of New York, came into my office one winter day with a parcel wrapped in brown paper. He announced that he had just returned from "down south," and had brought me a present. Now presents from Captain Curtis are something of an event and this was no exception. This time it turned out to be the Blue-bill shown in Plate No. 111, a decoy made by Captain Elijah Cobb, one time light tender of Cobbs Island Light, Virginia.

On information supplied by Captain Curtis, I later secured the Brant shown in Plate No. 112 also by Elijah Cobb. The heads are conventional yet the "driftwood" legend was completely substantiated. It will be noted that both decoys have cylindrical bodies, recalling "spars washed up on the beach" as per rumor. In spite of the spar-like bodies, both examples are very fine decoys.

But to return to the subject of dual painting. Here again is the combination of male and female plumage. A modification of both patterns is painted in a darkened brown—an interesting idea, more easily pictured than explained.

BACK BAY, VIRGINIA

As outlined in the first part of this section, decoys of the Chesapeake, are in general of normal size. On the Susquehanna Flats, the standards are maintained by the many units employed by the batteries. Other localities of the region seem to follow in their footsteps. On Back Bay, Virginia, however, and on down through Currituck Sound, the gunning of Canvas-back and Redhead is conducted over greatly oversized decoys. The object, of course, is the greater visibility of larger units. As the batteries of these waters use fewer decoys than northern rigs, it is possible to handle them.

On a recent visit to Back Bay I checked the dimensions of a special set of Canvas-back and Redhead made to the club's order by a western decoy factory a few years previous. The bodies were 16 inches long, 8 inches wide with a depth of just under 5 inches. Examination of other examples in the vicinity seemed to indicate that decoys of approximately these dimensions were something of a standard.

The first of these big lures, however, were not made in factories or even by established decoy makers. The idea was introduced many years ago by market shooters. Many examples of early origin are still to be found. For the most part they are roughly made, have a quality of their own and show a deep knowledge of water and waterfowl.

To better illustrate the transition, I show in Plate No. 2 comparison heads of the same vicinity. The head at the upper left gives the old and normal size Canvas-back, the one at the upper right, the normal Redhead. Both examples are the work of Mr. Lee Dudley, market gunner and decoy maker of Knotts Island, Virginia. The lower heads show the work of early gunners, forerunners of the increase in size later to be adopted by the entire region. Plate No. 3 shows one of the complete primitive decoys. The maker is unknown to me but it serves to illustrate the custom of oversize decoys in Back Bay. The body of this decoy is 16 inches long, 8 inches wide, with a depth of 4½ inches.

The examples used in this review of southern customs were gifts of my hosts at the Knotts Island Gun Club. During my stay there in 1930, several clubs, both on Back Bay and Currituck were visited, but time was limited. It is a region of great interest to the student of American wild fowling and literally alive with history. Protected by remoteness and still in the hands of natives and sportsmen, it will probably remain so for many years. At some time in the future I hope to explore it thoroughly; those romantic waters and shores of Back Bay, Currituck Sound and Albemarle Sound. When that time comes I will add to my collection of decoys.

REGIONAL DECOYS

CURRITUCK SOUND

It is curious how seemingly vague and unrelated events crystallize into definite and helpful reality. As applied to decoys one of these faint trails led finally to the acquisition of the Primitive Swan decoy from Currituck Sound shown in Plate No. 113.

In 1932 *The National Geographic Magazine* published an article on wild life by a well known sportsman-naturalist. Among the many photographic illustrations by the author, Mr. George Shiras, 3rd, there appeared a young Swan in the act of visiting a group of four crude Swan decoys. The photograph had been taken on Currituck Sound, North Carolina.*

Needless to say, I wrote Mr. Shiras and received a very interesting reply. In 1923 he had joined the Narrows Island Club, Poplar Branch, Currituck Co., N. C., largely for the purpose of photographing wild fowl. As a matter of record, I shall quote that part of his letter dealing with the Swan decoys.

"Before this time, 1923, and down to the present Swans have been given continuous protection and moreover this handsome bird was seldom shot in the earlier days by members of the various clubs and so Swan decoys were seldom seen. The ones you refer to were borrowed from an old market hunter at Poplar Branch, for many natives had a liking for young Swans. I think it was likely true that the long necks were attached to the body of geese decoys. They were very crude and the older Swans eyed them with suspicion."

At the end of his letter Mr. Shiras spoke of Swan decoys belonging to another club further north, as follows: "This club had a very handsome set of Swan decoys, each one a third larger than normal, so they were conspicuous a long distance."

The year following this correspondence with Mr. Shiras

* "Wild Life of the Atlantic and Gulf Coasts." A field naturalist's photographic record of nearly half a century of fruitful exploration. By George Shiras, 3rd.

I planned to visit this region but business intervened and I was unable to carry out my plans. Shortly after New Year's, however, I received an unexpected reminder, an ordinary flour barrel headed with burlap sacking. The outside bore a printed tag of the Narrows Island Club. Inside, spiked fast to the bulging staves was one of the straight necked Swan decoys shown in George Shiras' illustration.

This swan from Currituck was sent to me by the late Major Herman Foster Stone of New York, then a member of Narrows Island Club. Major Stone was an ardent sportsman of wide experience on southern waters. His knowledge and enjoyment of fowling will be long remembered. It was he who gave me the Sickle-billed Curlew with the forged iron bill, Plate No. 115. His cryptic note accompanying the gift is typical of much decoy history. "Old Sickle Bill. Found under an unoccupied house on Capers Island, South Carolina, (near Charleston). H. F. Stone."

GULF STATES

That great region lying south of the Carolinas and west along the Gulf of Mexico, has never gone in for native decoy making. Although using decoys to a considerable extent, the southern gunners relied on northern factories to supply them, principally those of the Middle West. In recent years the south has developed its own factories but the situation remains unchanged for there are practically no hand makers. Surprising but true.

On the other hand, I have always looked forward to finding decoys made by Seminole Indians or decoys of hand hewn cypress by denizens of the bayous along the Gulf States or the great marshes on the delta of the Mississippi. But no. So far, only factory stools and in recent years live decoys gradually displacing artificial lures.

There is, however, one exception: the Canada Geese "pro-

PLATE 109
OLD BLUE-BILL
Elkton, Md.

PLATE 110
WHISTLING SWAN
Eastern Shore of Maryland

PLATE 111
BLUE-BILL *by Capt. Elijah Cobb*
Cobb's Island, Va., 1860

PLATE 112
BRANT *by Capt. Elijah Cobb*
Cobb's Island, Va., 1860

files" used by gunners on the sand bars of the Mississippi River. These decoys are made locally and have been for many years. They are similar in every way to the "profiles" employed in the cut-over wheat fields of western states, made of wood, sheet iron or tin. The "stick-up" idea, of course, is very ancient; first employed by aborigines in killing waterfowl on land. The manner of adoption on southern gunning grounds cannot be definitely arrived at.

The absence of decoy making in the south, while hard for the northerner to understand, is explained by conditions. Birds were very plentiful and decoys much less of a necessity in the methods employed in taking them. Before recording my observations, however, I referred the matter to Mr. Nash Buckingham of Memphis, Tennessee. Mr. Buckingham is a sportsman of national reputation, well known through his writings on the subject of American fowling. Personally, I like to remember him as the author of that modern classic called *De Shootines' Gent'man*. His opinion on the southern decoy situation seems desirable and authoritative.

Plate No. 116 shows a sand bar in the Mississippi, a set of Geese profiles in position, and the gunner in the pit ready for callers. Here at the end, I shall quote his remarks which were given in answer to a query as to conditions in Gulf States and the Mississippi Valley. It is surprising that so little can be said of decoy making in a region so rich in waterfowl and tradition.

"Dear Mr. Barber:

This region, since I can remember, has relied on duck decoys of standard manufacture; gradually displaced, in the main, by the use of live decoys. A few swamp angels and Reelfoot and Big Lake guides of the old days blocked out stools, but I doubt if any are now in existence, and I have been around a bit regionally. For years, we've made our own goose decoys, profiles, in this part of the world. Beginning with heavy sheet-iron models; then light weight tin ones, hand painted. We also used wooden profiles, but they were bulky, and the bills chipped. In recent years we've used mostly the factory folding paper decoy, made in both the profile and the 'spread' type. I always repainted mine, however, because the stock models, while well done, were coated with water-proofing, a sort of paraffin, that shone badly in bright sunlight. So I used flat black, white and umber to dull 'em. . . . Since you've mentioned it, I'll look and ask around and if I run into anything in the way of goose or duck decoys, I'll send them on to you. Glad to co-operate, and don't hesitate to write me if I can help you.

NASH BUCKINGHAM.

May 31, 1934."

It would appear on this authority that the southern gunner, while a user, has never been a maker of decoys, or if so—none of them remain. At the same time, rules of this kind are subject to exception, and the exceptions are frequently of great distinction. So it would not surprise me at all some day to add to my collection an outstanding example of decoy making from this romantic region. I don't know where it will come from, perhaps the Father of Waters—or may be from deep in the Everglades of Florida. It is too much to ask of a collector to believe that fowlers of the deep south missed the great American impulse to make decoy ducks.

PLATE 113
PRIMITIVE SWAN, Narrows Island Club
Currituck Sound, N. C.

PLATE 114
FEMALE CANVAS-BACK
Currituck Sound, N. C., about 1880

PLATE 115
OLD SICKLE-BILLED CURLEW
Caper's Island, S. C.

PLATE 116
SET OF GOOSE PROFILES
Mississippi Sand-bar

XVIII

The Modern Decoy

To BEGIN A BOOK is a pleasurable undertaking, but to end a book is another matter; and by end—I mean to definitely and with finality achieve conclusion. At the start, supported by great enthusiasm, an approach is readily found, the pattern unfolds and subject expands. Fine. But the end is far away, indefinite and beyond the horizon. I for one gave no thought to it until confronted by conclusion itself. But having reached the end, the way, after all, seems clear. As a road to final exit, I shall make a decoy myself.

How this decoy is made has a new angle of approach. In the process of collecting, certain features of decoy design and construction have become of increasing importance. These features have not been contained in any one decoy, but scattered over many examples from many localities. In course of time these separate items have merged—assembled themselves into a single form. By showing this composite picture, I disclose my conclusion with respect to decoys. I call it the "modern decoy," and show not one but two: a puddle duck and a diving duck, but for the purpose of this discussion, of no particular species.

Upon critical examination, it will be seen that a decoy must be designed in such a way as to lie best at anchor, must be an inanimate but perfect buoy of species.

Material, construction and portraiture should be of such a nature as to stand up under the hard usage to which decoys are subject, also the trials imposed by amphibian existence.

The impression of plumage should be obtained by painted patterns that clearly convey species and sex, and capable of easy repainting.

If these abstract requirements are adhered to, the resultant decoy will be symbolic rather than naturalistic—a quiet, perfect buoy of species, in the protective coloring of nature.

Every one of these ideal features will be found incorporated in old examples, not once but many times. Never in my experience, however, have I seen them assembled in one single stool duck as in this composite decoy. The full deep breast comes from an Old Squaw toller as made by a New England fisherman. Parallel side lines of the body are adopted from the present day Canvas-back decoys as made at Havre de Grace, Maryland, a region using more decoys than all others put together. The flat bottom and long keel are taken from the cork decoys of the Great South Bay. In like fashion other practical features of old decoys have been used. Even the radical head fastening is not without precedent, for the cotter pin idea appears in a Maine Black Duck of my collection, the work of an Old Town Indian.

But how these and other features are assembled in one decoy is best seen by reference to the accompanying diagrams. These drawings were first laid out to embody and co-ordinate selected items of design and construction. Trial decoys were then made and drawings revised to incorporate features developed in process of actual making. In this respect, they reflect the models as shown in photographs.

Plate No. 119 shows a diving duck body with Canvas-back head and painting. Plate No. 120—a shoal water decoy, unpainted but with Black Duck head. The drawings are carefully dimensioned and made for working purposes. Both types of body are standard and designed to serve several species. For example, a Blue-bill head and Blue-bill painting when applied to the deep water body, makes the change; the same applies for

Redhead and Whistler. The shoal water body has the same flexibility. In every instance the standard hull with keel and mortise for head remains the same.

The diving duck body in Plate No. 119 is cut from a white pine block, three by six by twelve inches. The breast is a half circle. Side lines of hull are parallel and carried aft to the abrupt curve at the tail. Bottom lines converge slightly from the after quarter to preserve balance in the water. The bottom proper is flat, with slightly rounded edges. Keel is of oak, one and one-quarter inches deep by three-quarters inch wide and extends the full length of bottom. The longitudinal sections shows no overhang at the breast giving maximum length of water line; the cross section discloses minimum material cut away in shaping the back.

The head in Plate No. 119 is cut from one and one-half inch white pine or whitewood, and bored to receive a $\frac{5}{8}$ inch hard wood dowel. The fastening of the head has rather special features. Due to the swelling of wood when immersed in water and subsequent shrinkage when again dried out, the joint between head and body in present decoys is soon fractured. This expansion and contraction of material is largely responsible for the prevalence of broken necks in decoys after a single season of use. To overcome this breakage another method of construction is recommended.

Instead of the usual nailing from the top, the fastening of the head to body is made by the principle of mortise, tenon and pin. To prevent twisting, the base of the head is seated in a slot or mortise cut in the body as shown. The bottom of the mortise is pitched and left open at the forward end for the escape of water. The head is held in the mortise by a wooden pin through a hole in the extended head dowel as indicated on the diagram. Fastening of this kind permits material of both units to go and come independent of each other. The pin through the tenon, or real element of fastening, remains unaffected.

Further application of the composite method is shown in

Plate No. 120. For this design the body is cut from a white pine block three by six by fourteen and one-half inches long. Portraiture is accomplished and symbolized by the longer body and pointed tail, characteristic of the shoal water species. The same general feature of design and construction are adhered to. The full, half-round breast is retained, also the flat bottom, keel and long bearing fore and aft. Still following precedent, this decoy is of a modified hollow type. The body is dug out from the bottom for about half its total depth. Side walls are left about one inch in thickness. In this type of construction the slotted head is fastened by a brass screw from underneath. The screw provides ample reinforcement for the neck.

Innovation appears again in the bottom closure. Here a heavy cotton duck, set in white lead and fastened with copper tacks is recommended. In the decoy shown, deck canvas that has been processed in course of manufacture with linseed oil is employed. It is finished by painting two coats of lead and oil. Canvas treated in this way will last for many years, is very light in weight and not affected by contraction and expansion. While the decoy is in use the canvas is below the water line and cannot be punctured by shot. It also receives considerable protection from the longitudinal keel and may be further reinforced by a cross frame as indicated in the diagram.

Decoys of this construction and design have a combination of merits. The hull of substantially less material than usually employed has greater visibility than the round or dead rise bottom decoy. The point of greatest buoyancy is well forward as required to hold up the weight of the head and overcome the downward pull of the anchor line. When not in use, the turns of anchor line will not slip off the parallel sides and become fouled. The general shape is economical, practical and showy. The flat bottom buoys up, and the long keel holds to the wind. No weight is required to maintain its balance.

Decoys constructed along these lines can be easily produced if rough work is handled by machinery. For this purpose,

PLATE 117
MODERN CANVAS-BACK *by the Author*

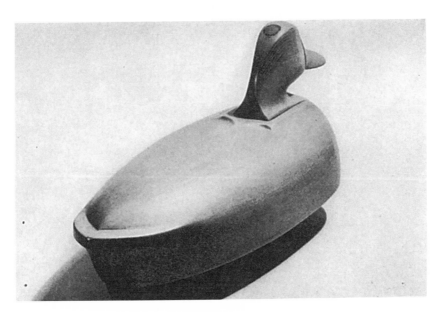

PLATE 118
MODERN BLACK DUCK *by the Author*

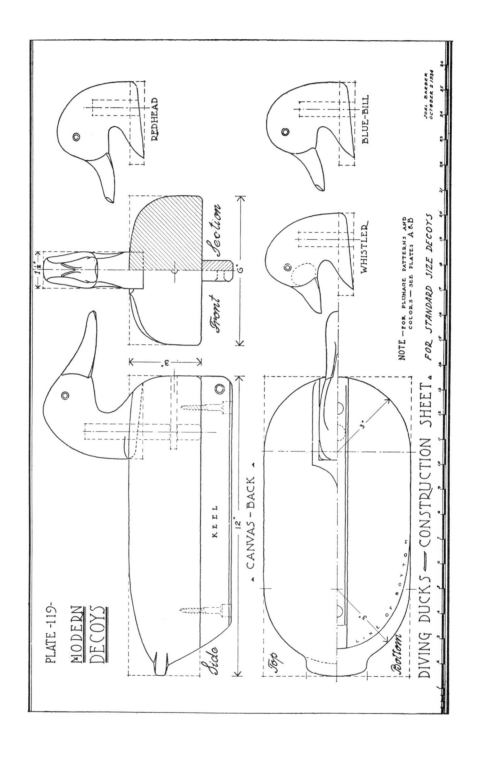

PLATE -119-

MODERN DECOYS

REDHEAD

BLUE-BILL

WHISTLER

Section

Front

Side

KEEL

CANVAS-BACK

Top

Bottom

LINE OF BOTTOM

NOTE — FOR PLUMAGE PATTERNS AND
COLORS SEE PLATES A & B

FOR STANDARD SIZE DECOYS

DIVING DUCKS — CONSTRUCTION SHEET.

JOEL BARBER
OCTOBER 2, 1934

standard equipment of the modern wood working mill is sufficient. Templates, cut from heavy Bristol Board, should be employed to lay out lines of body and head on the blocks. The body blocks, after marking, should be band sawed to exact shape and bored to receive the head dowel and cotter pin. The slot to receive the base of the head should also be cut to size and shape by a variety or dado machine. In the case of hollow decoys, the section to be removed should be cut away by a routing machine. It is better to do this branch of the work before, rather than after the body has been rounded to its final shape. Heads should be marked out, again using template, sawed to shape and bored to receive the ⅝ inch dowel. The overhead drill press will insure holes that will be plumb and true if laid out accurately. The same holds good for the slot to receive the head.

With the foregoing items taken care of by the mill, the work to be done by hand is greatly facilitated and uniformity of product assured. Again using a template the bottom shape of the body is laid out on the block and the process of final shaping begun. The exact section of rounded back is indicated by the diagram. The minor curves at the tail are accomplished by connecting top and bottom shapes by the fair sweeps indicated in the photograph.

The actual shaping of body is best accomplished by the use of a draw knife, and carried to conclusion with a spokeshave after the traditional fashion of making decoys by hand. Sandpaper should be used to remove tool marks.

Head making also goes back to the past. The sawn blocks, held in a vise, are roughly shaped with a draw knife, whittled to final form and sandpapered. The long head dowel should be set in white lead with the top finished flush with the top of the head. When the head is finally fitted and seated in its mortise, the projecting tenon should be bored to correspond with the pin location in the body. It is advisable to have this hole slightly larger than the pin. To complete the permanent fastening the pin is set in white lead and the end cut off flush with the breast.

The accompanying photographs of these decoys show features not apparent in the projected plans of top and sides. The views were purposely taken to disclose the shape of the body. The exact process of making heads is difficult to convey by description. Beyond the pattern of outline, the use of a good model is strongly recommended.

The same difficulty is true of painting decoys. Any practical painter can give formulae for mixing paint, but what to paint requires expert knowledge. To those who have this knowledge, instruction is offensive. To those without, the use of models is again advised.

There is one more feature of decoy making that is properly a part of the modern problem; the necessity of better decoys, and decoys of variety. It is well known that in groups of birds assembled on water, uniformity of pose is rare. The nearest approach to sameness occurs only at moments of alarm or of curiosity preceding alarm. Where a large number of decoys are used, therefore, a variation of pose is strongly recommended. The value of this is expressed by the singular and desirable animation of old rigs composed of decoys from different sources. We have all seen such assemblages, home made decoys, factory decoys, decoys purloined, and derelicts picked up on the beach. Good, bad and cock-eyed, but in formation, producing a very desirable effect.

To accomplish this feature, a variety of head poses or shapes is strongly recommended. A few snugged down heads may be employed along with other modifications of the standard shape. In general, however, it is well to keep heads rather high to avoid bills icing up during freezing weather. When this happens, the decoys ride down at the head in dull and unnatural manner.

In a general study of the subject, I have found that decoys are becoming of increasing importance to the modern sports-

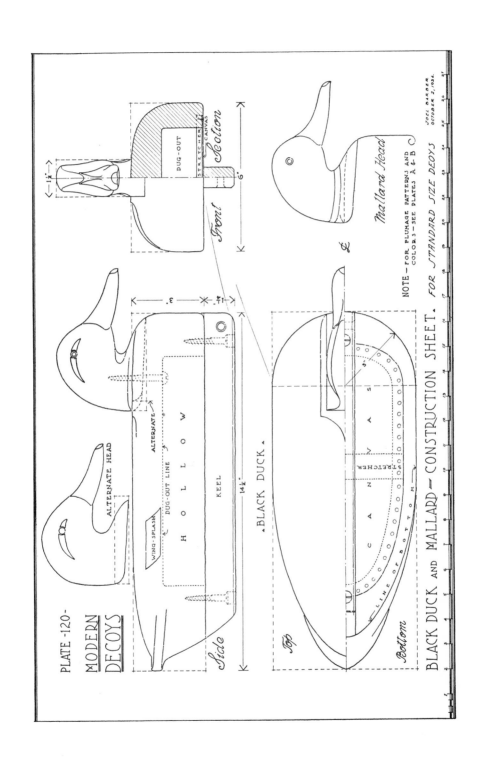

PLATE -120-

MODERN DECOYS

ALTERNATE HEAD

HOLLOW

WING-SPLASH

DUG-OUT LINE

ALTERNATE

KEEL

Side

Front

Bottom

DUG-OUT

STRETCHER

CANVAS

Mallard Head

Top

C A N V A S

STRETCHER

LINE OF BOTTOM

Bottom

BLACK DUCK

BLACK DUCK AND MALLARD — CONSTRUCTION SHEET. FOR STANDARD SIZE DECOYS

NOTE — FOR PLUMAGE PATTERNS AND
COLORS — SEE PLATES A & B

JOEL BARBER
OCTOBER 2, 1934.

man. Formerly relegated to the hands of professionals, they now appear as an item of personal equipment. This may be due to the scarcity of birds and consequent need of better decoys; or may have rise in a growing interest in decoys themselves. Whatever the source, the modern sportsman is becoming decoy conscious. Here and there also, is a man who makes his own decoys. To him these observations on present day methods are addressed.

And so concludes my story. Indian bird lures of primitive America at the beginning, modern decoys at the end. Between the two extremes lie a thousand years and many decoy makers. Presumably there will be others to carry on the tradition. What they will make—remains to be seen.